DRAMATIS PERSONÆ

DEMIPHO,[1] Aged Athenians, brothers.
CHREMES,[2]
ANTIPHO,[3] son of Demipho.
PHÆDRIA,[4] son of Chremes.
PHORMIO,[5] a Parasite.
GETA,[6] servant of Demipho.
DAVUS,[7] a servant.
HEGIO,[8] Advocate.
CRATINUS,[9] Advocate.
CRITO,[10] Advocate
DORIO,[11] a Procurer.
NAUSISTRATA,[12] the wife of Chremes.
SOPHRONA,[13] the nurse of Phanium.

SCENE:—Athens; before the houses of Demipho, Chremes, and Dorio.

THE SUBJECT

Chremes and Demphio are two aged Athenians, brothers. Nausistrata, the wife of Chremes, is a wealthy woman, possessed of large estates in the island of Lemnos. Chremes, who goes thither yearly to receive the rents, meets with a poor woman there, whom he secretly marries, and has by her a daughter called Phanium: while engaged in this intrigue, Chremes passes at Lemnos by the name of Stilpho. By his wife, Nausistrata, at Athens, Chremes has a son, named Phædria, and his brother has a son, named Antipho. Phanium having now arrived at her fifteenth year, the two brothers privately agree that she shall be brought to Athens and married to Antipho. For this purpose, Chremes goes to Lemnos, while Demipho is obliged to take a journey to Cilicia. On departing, they leave their sons in the care of Geta, one of Demipho's servants. Shortly afterward, Phædria falls in love with a Music-girl, but, from want of means, is unable to purchase her from her owner. In the mean time, the Lemnian wife of Chremes, urged by poverty, embarks for Athens, whither she arrives with her daughter and her nurse. Here they inquire for Stilpho, but in vain, as they can not find any one of that name. Shortly after, the mother dies, and Antipho, seeing Phanium by accident, falls in love with her. Being wishful to marry her, he applies to Phormio, a Parasite, for his advice. The latter hits upon the following scheme: there being a law at Athens, which obliges the next-of-kin to female orphans, either to marry them or give them a portion, the Parasite pretends that he is a friend of Phanium, and insists that Antipho is her nearest relation, and is consequently bound to marry her. Antipho is summoned before a court of justice, and it being previously arranged, allows judgment to be given against himself, and immediately marries Phanium. Shortly after, the old men return upon the same day, and are much vexed, the one on finding that his son has married a woman without a fortune, the other that he has lost the opportunity of getting his daughter advantageously married. In the mean time, Phædria being necessitated to raise some money to purchase the Music-girl, Geta and Phormio arrange that the former shall pretend to the old man that Phormio has consented to take back the woman whom Antipho has married, if Demipho will give her a portion of

Phormio (The Scheming Parasite) by Terence

A Translation by Henry Thomas Riley

Publius Terentius Afer is better known to us as the Roman playwright, Terence.

Much of his life, especially the early part, is either unknown or has conflicting sources and accounts.

His birth date is said to be either 185 BC or a decade earlier: 195 BC. His place of birth is variously listed as in, or, near Carthage, or, in Greek Italy to a woman taken to Carthage as a slave. It is suggested that he lived in the territory of the Libyan tribe that the Romans called Afri, near Carthage, before being brought to Rome as a slave. Probability suggests that it was there, in North Africa, several decades after the destruction of Carthage by the Romans in 146 BC, at the end of the Punic Wars, that Terence spent his early years.

One reliable fact is that he was sold to P. Terentius Lucanus, a Roman senator, who had him educated and, impressed by his literary talents, freed him.

These writing talents were to ensure his legacy as a playwright down through the millennia. His comedies, partially adapted from Greek plays of the late phases of Attic Comedy, were performed for the first time around 170–160 BC. All six of the plays he has known to have written have survived.

Indeed, thanks to his simple conversational Latin, which was both entertaining and direct, Terence's works were heavily used by monasteries and convents during the Middle Ages and The Renaissance. Scribes often learned Latin through the copious copying of Terence's texts. Priests and nuns often learned to speak Latin through re-enactment of Terence's plays. Although his plays often dealt with pagan material, the quality and distinction of his language promoted the copying and preserving of his text by the church. This preservation enabled his work to influence a wide spectrum of later Western drama.

When he was 25 (or 35 depending on which year of birth you ascribe too), Terence travelled to Greece but never returned. It has long been assumed that he died at some point during the journey.

Of his own family nothing is known, except that he fathered a daughter and left a small but valuable estate just outside Rome.

His most famous quotation reads: "Homo sum, humani nihil a me alienum puto", or "I am human, and I think nothing human is alien to me."

Index of Contents

thirty minae. Demipho borrows the money of Chremes, and pays it to Phormio, who hands it over to Phædria, and Phædria to Dorio, for his mistress. At this conjuncture, it becomes known who Phanium really is, and the old men are delighted to find that Antipho has married the very person they wished. They attempt, however, to get back the thirty minae from Phormio, and proceed to threats and violence. On this, Phormio, who has accidentally learned the intrigue of Chremes with the woman of Lemnos, exposes him, and relates the whole story to his wife, Nausistrata; on which she censures her husband for his bad conduct, and the Play concludes with her thanks to Phormio for his information.

THE TITLE OF THE PLAY

Performed at the Roman Games,[14] L. Posthumius Albinus and L. Cornelius Merula being Curule Ædiles. L. mbivius Turpio and L. Atilius Prænestinus performed it. Flaccus, the freedman of Claudius, composed the music to a base and a treble flute. It is wholly from the Greek, being the Epidicazomenos of Apollodorus. It was represented four times,[15] C. Fannius and M. Valerius being Consuls.[16]

PHORMIO; OR, THE SCHEMING PARASITE

THE SUMMARY OF C. SULPITIUS APOLLINARIS

Demipho, the brother of Chremes, has gone abroad, his son Antipho being left at Athens. Chremes has secretly a wife and a daughter at Lemnos, another wife at Athens, and an only son, who loves a Music-girl. The mother arrives at Athens from Lemnos, and there dies. The girl, her orphan daughter, (Chemes being away,) arranges the funeral. After Antipho has fallen in love with her when seen there, through the aid of the Parasite he receives her as his wife. His father and Chremes, having now returned, begin to be enraged. Afterward they give thirty minæ to the Parasite, that he may take her as his own wife. With this money the Music-girl is bought for Phædria. Antipho then keeps his wife, who has been recognized by his uncle.

THE PROLOGUE

Since the old Poet[17] can not withdraw our bard from his pursuits and reduce him to indolence, he endeavors, by invectives, to deter him from writing: for he is wont to say to this effect,— that the Plays which he has hitherto composed are poor in their language, and of meagre style: because he has nowhere described a frantic youth as seeing a hind in flight, and the hounds pursuing; while he implores[18] and entreated that he would give her aid. But if he had been aware that his Play, when formerly first represented, stood its ground more through the merits of the performers than its own, he would attack with much less boldness than he does. Now, if there is any one who says or thinks to this effect, that if the old Poet had not assailed him first, the young one could have devised no Prologue for him to repeat, without having some one to abuse, let him receive this for an answer: "that the prize is proposed in common to all who apply to the Dramatic art." He has aimed at driving our Poet from his studies to absolute want; he then has intended this for an answer, not an attack. If he had opposed him with fair words, he would have heard himself civilly addressed; what has been given by him, let him consider as now returned. I will make an end of speaking about him, when, of his own accord, he himself makes an end of offending. Now give your attention to what I request. I present you a new play, which they call "Epidicazomenos,"[19] in Greek: in the Latin, he calls it "Phormio;" because the person that acts the principal part is Phormio, a Parasite, through whom, principally, the plot will be carried on, if your favor attends the Poet. Lend your attention; in silence give an ear with impartial feelings, that we may not experience a like fortune to what we did, when, through a tumult, our Company was driven from the place;[20] which place, the merit of the actor, and your good-will and candor seconding it, has since restored unto us.

ACT THE FIRST

SCENE I

Enter **DAVUS**,[21] with a bag of money in his hand.

DAVUS
Geta, my very good friend and fellow-townsman, came to me yesterday. There had been for some time a trifling balance of money of his in my hands upon a small account; he asked me to make it up. I have done so, and am carrying it to him. But I hear that his master's son has taken a wife; this, I suppose, is scraped together as a present for her. How unfair a custom!—that those who have the least should always be giving something to the more wealthy! That which the poor wretch has with difficulty spared, ounce by ounce, out of his allowance,[22] defrauding himself of every indulgence, the whole of it will she carry off, without thinking with how much labor it has been acquired. And then besides, Geta will be struck[23] for another present[24] when his mistress is brought to bed; and then again for another present, when the child's birthday comes; when they initiate him,[25] too: all this the mother will carry off; the child will only be the pretext for the present. But don't I see Geta there?

SCENE II

Enter **GETA**, from the house of **DEMIPHO**.

GETA [At the door, to those within]
If any red-haired man should inquire for me—

DAVUS [Stepping forward]
Here he is, say no more.

GETA [Starting]
Oh! Why I was trying to come and meet you, Davus.

DAVUS [Giving the money to **GETA**]
Here, take it; it's all ready counted out;[26] the number just amounts to the sum I owed you.

GETA
I am obliged to you; and I return you thanks for not having forgotten me.

DAVUS

Especially as people's ways are nowadays; things are come to such a pass, if a person repays you any thing, you must be greatly obliged to him. But why are you out of spirits?

GETA

What, I? You little know what terror and peril I am in.

DAVUS

What's the matter?

GETA

You shall know, if you can only keep it secret.

DAVUS

Out upon you, simpleton; the man, whose trustworthiness you have experienced as to money, are you afraid to intrust with words? In what way have I any interest in deceiving you?

GETA

Well then, listen.

DAVUS

I give you my best attention.

GETA

Davus, do you know Chremes, the elder brother of our old gentleman?

DAVUS

Why should I not?

GETA

Well, and his son Phædria?

DAVUS

As well as your own self.

GETA

It so happened to both the old gentlemen, just at the same period, that the one had to take a journey to Lemnos, and our old man to Cilicia, to see an old acquaintance; he tempted over the old man by letters, promising him all but mountains of gold.

DAVUS
To one who had so much property, that he had more than he could use?

GETA
Do have done; that is his way.

DAVUS
Oh, as for that, I really ought to have been a man of fortune.

GETA
When departing hence, both the old gentlemen left me as a sort of tutor to their sons.

DAVUS
Ah, Geta, you undertook a hard task there.

GETA
I came to experience it, I know that. I'm quite sure that I was forsaken by my good Genius, who must have been angry with me.[27] I began to oppose them at first; but what need of talking? As long as I was trusty to the old men, I was paid for it in my shoulder-blades. This, then, occurred to my mind: why, this is folly to kick against the spur.[28] I began to do every thing for them that they wished to be humored in.

DAVUS
You knew how to make your market.[29]

GETA
Our young fellow did no mischief whatever at first; that Phædria at once picked up a certain damsel, a Music-girl, and fell in love with her to distraction. She belonged to a most abominable Procurer; and their fathers had taken good care that they should have nothing to give him. There remained nothing for him then but to feed his eyes, to follow her about, to escort her to the school,[30] and to escort her back again. We, having nothing to do, lent our aid to Phædria. Near the school at which she was taught, right opposite the place, there was a certain barber's shop: here we were generally in the habit of waiting for her, until she was

coming home again. In the mean time, while one day we were sitting there, there came in a young man in tears;[31] we were surprised at this. We inquired what was the matter? "Never," said he, "has poverty appeared to me a burden so grievous and so insupportable as just now. I have just seen a certain poor young woman in this neighborhood lamenting her dead mother. She was laid out before her, and not a single friend, acquaintance, or relation was there with her, except one poor old woman, to assist her in the funeral: I pitied her. The girl herself was of surpassing beauty." What need of a long story? She moved us all. At once Antipho exclaims, "Would you like us to go and visit her?" The other said, "I think we ought— let us go— show us the way, please." We went, and arrived there; we saw her; the girl was beautiful, and that you might say so the more, there was no heightening to her beauty; her hair disheveled, her feet bare, herself neglected, and in tears; her dress mean, so that, had there not been an excess of beauty in her very charms, these circumstances must have extinguished those charms. The one who had lately fallen in love with the Music-girl said: "She is well enough;" but our youth—

DAVUS
I know it already— fell in love with her.

GETA
Can you imagine to what an extent? Observe the consequence. The day after, he goes straight to the old woman; entreats her to let him have her: she, on the other hand, refuses him, and says that he is not acting properly; that she is a citizen of Athens, virtuous, and born of honest parents: that if he wishes to make her his wife, he is at liberty to do so according to law; but if otherwise, she gives him a refusal. Our youth was at a loss what to do. He was both eager to marry her, and he dreaded his absent father.

DAVUS
Would not his father, if he had returned, have given him leave?

GETA
He let him marry a girl with no fortune, and of obscure birth! He would never do so.

DAVUS

What came of it at last?

GETA
What came of it? There is one Phormio here, a Parasite, a fellow of great assurance; may all the Gods confound him!

DAVUS
What has he done?

GETA
He has given this piece of advice, which I will tell you of. "There is a law, that orphan girls are to marry those who are their next-of-kin; and the same law commands such persons to marry them. I'll say you are the next-of-kin, and take out a summons[32] against you; I'll pretend that I am a friend of the girl's father; we will come before the judges: who her father was, who her mother, how she is related to you— all this I'll trump up, just as will be advantageous and suited to my purpose; on your disproving none of these things, I shall prevail, of course. Your father will return; a quarrel will be the consequence; what care I? She will still be ours."

DAVUS
An amusing piece of assurance!

GETA
He was persuaded to this. It was carried out; they came into court: we were beaten. He has married her.

DAVUS
What is it you tell me?

GETA
Just what you have heard.

DAVUS
O Geta, what will become of you?

GETA
Upon my faith, I don't know; this one thing I do know, whatever fortune may bring, I'll bear it with firmness.

DAVUS

You please me; well, that is the duty of a man.

GETA

All my hope is in myself.

DAVUS

I commend you.

GETA

Suppose I have recourse to some one to intercede for me, who will plead for me in these terms: "Pray, do forgive him this time; but if after this he does any thing, I make no entreaty:" if only he doesn't add, "When I've gone, e'en kill him for my part."

DAVUS

What of the one who was usher to the Music-girl?[33]

GETA [Shrugging his shoulders]

So so, but poorly.

DAVUS

Perhaps he hasn't much to give.

GETA

Why, really, nothing at all, except mere hopes.

DAVUS

Is his father come back or not?

GETA

Not yet.

DAVUS

Well, when do you expect your old man?

GETA

I don't know for certain; but I just now heard that a letter has been brought from him, and has been left with the officers of the customs: I'm going to fetch it.

DAVUS
Is there any thing else that you want with me, Geta?

GETA
Nothing; but that I wish you well.

[Exit **DAVUS**.

Hark you, boy—
[Calling at the door]
—Is nobody coming out here?

[A **LAD** comes out.

Take this, and give it to Dorcium.

[He gives the purse to the **LAD**, who carries it into **DEMIPHO'S** house and exit **GETA**.

SCENE III

Enter **ANTIPHO** and **PHÆDRIA**.

ANTIPHO
That things should have come to such a pass, Phædria, that I should be in utter dread of my father, who wishes me so well, whenever his return comes into my thoughts! Had I not been inconsiderate, I might have waited for him, as I ought to have done.

PHÆDRIA
What's the matter?

ANTIPHO

Do you ask the question? You, who have been my confederate in so bold an adventure? How I do wish it had never entered the mind of Phormio to persuade me to this, or to urge me in the heat of my passion to this step, which is the source of my misfortunes. Then I should not have obtained her; in that case I might have been uneasy for some few days; but still, this perpetual anxiety would not have been tormenting my mind.

[Touching **PHÆDRIA**.

PHÆDRIA
I hear you.

ANTIPHO
While I am every moment expecting his return, who is to sever from me this connection.[34]

PHÆDRIA
Other men feel uneasiness because they can not gain what they love; you complain because you have too much. You are surfeited with love, Antipho. Why, really, upon my faith, this situation of yours is surely one to be coveted and desired. So may the Gods kindly bless me, could I be at liberty to be so long in possession of the object of my love, I could contentedly die. Do you, then, form a judgment as to the rest, what I am now suffering from this privation, and what pleasure you enjoy from the possession of your desires; not to mention how, without any expense, you have obtained a well-born and genteel woman, and have got a wife of unblemished reputation: happy you, were not this one thing wanting, a mind capable of bearing all this with moderation. If you had to deal with that Procurer with whom I have to deal, then you would soon be sensible of it. We are mostly all of us inclined by nature to be dissatisfied with our lot.

ANTIPHO
Still, on the other hand, Phædria, you now seem to me the fortunate man, who still have the liberty, without restraint, of resolving on what pleases you best: whether to keep, to love on, or to give her up. I, unfortunately, have got myself into that position, that I have neither right[35] to give her up, nor liberty to retain her. But how's this? Is it our Geta I see running this way? 'Tis he himself. Alas! I'm dreadfully afraid what news it is he's now bringing me.

Enter **GETA**, running, at the other side of the stage.

GETA [To himself]
Geta, you are undone, unless you instantly find out some expedient; so suddenly do such mighty evils now threaten me thus unprepared, which I neither know how to shun, nor how to extricate myself therefrom; for this daring step of ours can not now any longer be kept a secret. If such a result is not adroitly guarded against, these matters will cause the ruin of myself, or of my master.

ANTIPHO [To **PHÆDRIA**]
Why, I wonder, is he coming in such fright?

GETA [To himself]
Besides, I've but a moment left for this matter— my master's close at hand.

ANTIPHO [To **PHÆDRIA**]
What mischief is this?

GETA [To himself]
When he comes to hear of it, what remedy shall I discover for his anger? Am I to speak? I shall irritate him: be silent? I shall provoke him: excuse myself? I should be washing a brickbat.[36] Alas! unfortunate me! While I am trembling for myself, this Antipho distracts my mind. I am concerned for him; I'm in dread for him: 'tis he that now keeps me here; for had it not been for him, I should have made due provision for my safety, and have taken vengeance on the old man for his crabbedness; I should have scraped up something, and straightway taken to my heels away from here.

ANTIPHO [To **PHÆDRIA**]
I wonder what running away or theft it is that he's planning.

GETA [To himself]

But where shall I find Antipho, or which way go look for him?

PHÆDRIA [To **ANTIPHO**]
He's mentioning your name.

ANTIPHO [To **PHÆDRIA**]
I know not what great misfortune I expect to hear from this messenger.

PHÆDRIA [To **ANTIPHO**]
Why, are you in your senses?

GETA [To himself]
I'll make my way homeward; he's generally there.

PHÆDRIA [To **ANTIPHO**]
Let's call the fellow back.

ANTIPHO [Calling out]
Stop, this instant.

GETA [Turning round]
Heyday— with authority enough, whoever you are.

ANTIPHO
Geta!

GETA
The very person I wanted to find.

ANTIPHO
Pray, tell me what news you bring and dispatch it in one word, if you can.

GETA
I'll do so.

ANTIPHO
Out with it.

GETA
Just now, at the harbor—

ANTIPHO
What, my father—?

GETA
You've hit it.

ANTIPHO
Ruined outright!

PHÆDRIA
Pshaw!

ANTIPHO
What am I to do?

PHÆDRIA [To **GETA**]
What is it you say?

GETA
That I have seen his father, your uncle.

ANTIPHO
How am I, wretch that I am, now to find a remedy for this sudden misfortune? But if it should be my fortune, Phanium, to be torn away from you, life would cease to be desirable.

GETA
Therefore, Antipho, since matters are thus, the more need have you to be on your guard; fortune helps the brave.

ANTIPHO
I am not myself.

GETA
But just now it is especially necessary you should be so, Antipho; for if your father perceives that you are alarmed, he will think that you have been guilty of some fault.

PHÆDRIA

That's true.

ANTIPHO
I can not change.

GETA
What would you do, if now something else still more difficult had to be done by you?

ANTIPHO
As I am not equal to this, I should be still less so to the other.

GETA
This is doing nothing at all, Phædria, let's be gone; why do we waste our time here to no purpose. I shall be off.

PHÆDRIA
And I too.

[They move as if going.

ANTIPHO
Pray, now, if I assume an air, will that do?

[He endeavors to assume another air.

GETA
You are trifling.

ANTIPHO
Look at my countenance— there's for you.
[Assuming a different air]
Will that do?

GETA
No.

ANTIPHO [Assuming another air]
Well, will this?

GETA

Pretty well.

ANTIPHO [Assuming a still bolder air]
Well then, this?

GETA

That's just the thing. There now, keep to that, and answer him word for word, like for like; don't let him, in his anger, disconcert you with his blustering words.

ANTIPHO

I understand.

GETA

Say that you were forced against your will by law, by sentence of the court; do you take me?

[Looking earnestly in one direction.

But who is the old man that I see at the end of the street?

ANTIPHO

'Tis he himself. I can not stand it.

[Going.

GETA

Oh! What are you about? Whither are you going, Antipho? Stop, I tell you.

ANTIPHO

I know my own self and my offense; to your management I trust Phanium and my own existence.

[Exit hastily.

SCENE V

PHÆDRIA and **GETA**.

PHÆDRIA
Geta, what's to be done now?

GETA
You will just hear some harsh language: I shall be trussed up and trounced, if I am not somewhat mistaken. But what we were just now advising Antipho to do, the same we must do ourselves, Phædria.

PHÆDRIA
Away with your "musts;" rather do you command me what I am to do.

GETA
Do you remember what were your words formerly on our entering upon this project, with the view of protecting yourselves from ill consequences— that their cause was just, clear, unanswerable, and most righteous?

PHÆDRIA
I remember it.

GETA
Well then, now there's need of that plea, or of one still better and more plausible, if such there can be.

PHÆDRIA
I'll use my best endeavors.

GETA
Do you then accost him first; I'll be here in reserve,[37] by way of reinforcement, if you give ground at all.

PHÆDRIA
Very well.

[They retire to a distance.

Enter **DEMIPHO**, at the other side of the stage.

DEMIPHO [To himself]
And is it possible that Antipho has taken a wife without my consent? and that no authority of mine— but let alone "authority"[38]— no displeasure of mine, at all events, has he been in dread of? To have no sense of shame! O audacious conduct! O Geta, rare adviser!

GETA [Apart to **PHÆDRIA**] Just brought in at last.

DEMIPHO
What will they say to me, or what excuse will they find? I wonder much.

GETA [Apart]
Why, I've found that out already; do think of something else.

DEMIPHO
Will he be saying this to me: "I did it against my will; the law compelled me?" I hear you, and admit it.

GETA [Apart]
Well said!

DEMIPHO
But knowingly, in silence, to give up the cause to his adversaries— did the law oblige him to do that as well?

GETA [Apart]
That is a hard blow.

PHÆDRIA
I'll clear that up; let me alone for that.

DEMIPHO
It is a matter of doubt what I am to do; for beyond expectation, and quite past all belief, has this befallen me. So enraged am I, that I can not compose my mind to think upon it. Wherefore it is the duty of all persons, when affairs are the most prosperous,[39] then in especial to reflect

within themselves in what way they are to endure adversity. Returning from abroad, let him always picture to himself dangers and losses, either offenses committed by a son, or the death of his wife, or the sickness of a daughter,— that these things are the common lot, so that no one of them may ever come as a surprise upon his feelings. Whatever falls out beyond his hopes, all that he must look upon as so much gain.

GETA [Apart]
O Phædria, it is incredible how much I surpass my master in wisdom. All my misfortunes have been already calculated upon by me, upon my master coming home. I must grind at the mill, be beaten, wear fetters, be set to work in the fields; not one individual thing of these will happen unexpected by my mind. Whatever falls out beyond my expectations, all that I shall look upon as so much gain. But why do you hesitate to accost him, and soften him at the outset with fair words?

[**PHÆDRIA** goes forward to accost **DEMIPHO**.

DEMIPHO [To himself]
I see Phædria, my brother's son, coming toward me.

PHÆDRIA
My uncle, welcome!

DEMIPHO
Greetings to you; but where is Antipho?

PHÆDRIA
That you have arrived in safety—

DEMIPHO
I believe it; answer my question.

PHÆDRIA
He is well; he's close at hand; but is every thing quite to your wishes?

DEMIPHO
I wish it was so, indeed.

PHÆDRIA

What's the matter?

DEMIPHO
Do you ask me, Phædria? You people have cooked up a fine marriage in my absence.

PHÆDRIA
What now, are you angry with him for that?

GETA [Apart]
What a clever contriver!

DEMIPHO
Have I not reason to be angry with him? I long for him to come into my sight, that he may know that through his faultiness, from being a mild father, I am become a most severe one.

PHÆDRIA
But he has done nothing, uncle, for which you should blame him.

DEMIPHO
Now, do look at that; all alike; all hanging together; when you know one, you know all.

PHÆDRIA
That is not the case.

DEMIPHO
When the one is in fault, the other is at hand to defend him; when it is the other, then he is ready; they just help one another by turns.

GETA [Apart]
The old man, without knowing it, has exactly described their proceedings.

DEMIPHO
For if it had not been so, you would not, Phædria, have stood up for him.

PHÆDRIA
If, uncle, it is the fact, that Antipho has been guilty of any fault, in consequence of which he has been too regardless of his interest or his

reputation, I would not allege any reason why he should not suffer what he deserves. But if some one by chance, relying upon his own artfulness, has laid a snare for our youthful age, and has succeeded, is it our fault or that of the judges, who often, through envy, take away from the rich, or, through compassion, award to the poor?

GETA [Apart]
Unless I knew the case, I could fancy he was saying the truth.

DEMIPHO
Is there any judge who can possibly know your rights, when you yourself don't answer a word— as he has done?

PHÆDRIA
He acted the part of an ingenuous young man; after they had come before the judges, he was not able to say what he had intended, so much did his modesty confuse him there through his bashfulness.

GETA [Apart]
I commend him: but why do I hesitate at once to accost the old man?
[Going forward to **DEMIPHO**]
Master, welcome to you! I'm glad to see you safe returned.

DEMIPHO [Ironically]
Ah, excellent guardian! save you, stay of my family, no doubt, to whom, at my departure, I intrusted my son.

GETA
For some minutes past I've heard you accusing all of us undeservedly; and me the most undeservedly of them all; for what would you have had me do for you in this affair? The laws do not allow a person who is a slave to plead; nor is there any giving evidence[40] on his part.

DEMIPHO
I grant all that: I admit this too— the young man, unused to courts, was bashful; I allow it: you, too, are a slave: still, if she was ever so near a relative, it was not necessary for him to marry her, but as the law enjoins, you might have given her a portion;[41] she could have looked out for another husband. Why, then, in preference, did he bring a pauper home?

GETA

No particular reason; but he hadn't the money.

DEMIPHO

He might have borrowed it from some person or other.

GETA

From some person or other? Nothing more easily said.

DEMIPHO

After all, if on no other terms, on interest.

GETA

Aye, aye, fine talking; as if any one would have trusted him, while you were living.[42]

DEMIPHO

No, it shall not be so; it must not be. Ought I to allow her to remain with him as his wife a single day? She merits no indulgence. I should like this fellow to be pointed out to me, or to be shown where he lives.

GETA

Phormio, do you mean?

DEMIPHO

That fellow, the woman's next friend?[43]

GETA

I'll have him here immediately.

DEMIPHO

Where is Antipho at present?

GETA

Away from home.

DEMIPHO

Go, Phædria, look for him, and bring him here.

PHÆDRIA

I'll go straightway to the place.

GETA [Aside]
To Pamphila, you mean.

[Exeunt **PHÆDRIA** and **GETA**.

SCENE VII

DEMIPHO, alone.

DEMIPHO [To himself]
I'll just step home to salute the household Gods.[44] From there, I'll go to the Forum, and summon some of my friends to give me their assistance in this affair; so that I may not be unprepared, when Phormio comes.

[Goes into his house.

ACT THE SECOND

SCENE I

Enter **PHORMIO** and **GETA**.

PHORMIO
And so you say[45] that, dreading his father's presence, he has taken himself off?

GETA
Exactly so.

PHORMIO
That Phanium is left alone?

GETA
Just so.

PHORMIO
And that the old man is in a rage?

GETA
Extremely so.

PHORMIO
The whole business, Phormio, rests on yourself alone; you yourself have hashed it up;[46] it must all be swallowed by yourself, so set about it.

GETA
I entreat you—

PHORMIO [To himself]
If he inquires.

GETA
In you is all our hope.

PHORMIO [To himself]
Look at this, now:— What if he sends her back?

GETA
It was you that urged us.

PHORMIO [To himself]
I think that will do.

GETA
Do help us.

PHORMIO [With alacrity]
Let the old gentleman come; all my plans are now ready prepared in my mind.

GETA
What will you do?

PHORMIO

What would you have me? But that Phanium may continue with him, and that I may clear Antipho from this charge, and turn upon myself[47] all the wrath of the old gentleman?

GETA
O brave and kind man! But, Phormio, I often dread lest this courage may end in the stocks at last.[48]

PHORMIO
Oh, by no means; I've made trial, and have already pondered on the paths for my feet. How many men before to-day do you suppose I have beaten, even to death, strangers as well as citizens: the better I understand it, the oftener I try it. Just tell me, look you, did you ever hear of an action of damages being brought against me?

GETA
How is that?

PHORMIO
Because the net is never spread for the hawk or the kite, that do us the mischief; it is spread for those that do us none: because in the last there is profit, while with the others it is labor lost. For persons, out of whom any thing can be got, there's risk from others; they know that I've got nothing. You will say: "They will take you,[49] when sentenced, into their house;" they have no wish to maintain a devouring fellow; and, in my opinion, they are wise, if for an injury they are unwilling to return the highest benefits.

GETA
It's impossible that sufficient thanks can be returned you by him for your kindness.

PHORMIO
Why no; no person can return thanks sufficient to his patron[50] for his kindness. For you to take your place at table at free cost,[51] anointed and just washed at the bath, with your mind at ease, whereas he is devoured with the care and expense: while every thing is being done to give you delight, he is being vexed at heart; you are laughing away, first to drink,[52] take the higher place; a banquet full of doubts[53] is placed before you—

GETA

What is the meaning of that expression?

PHORMIO

When you are in doubt which in especial to partake of. When you enter upon a consideration how delicious these things are, and how costly they are, the person who provides them, must you not account him a very God— neither more nor less?

GETA

The old man is coming; take care what you are about; the first onset is the fiercest; if you stand that, then, afterward, you may play just as you please.

[They retire to a distance.

SCENE II

Enter, at a distance, **DEMIPHO**, **HEGIO**, **CRATINUS**, and **CRITO**, following him.

DEMIPHO

Well now— did you ever hear of an injury being done to any person in a more affronting manner than this has to me? Assist me, I do beg of you.

GETA [Apart]
He's in a passion.

PHORMIO [Apart]
Do you mind your cue; I'll rouse him just now.
[Stepping forward and crying aloud]
Oh immortal Gods! does Demipho deny that Phanium here is related to him?

GETA
He does deny it.

DEMIPHO [To his **FRIENDS**]

I believe it is the very man I was speaking about. Follow me.

[They all come forward.

PHORMIO [To **GETA**]

And that he knows who her father was?

GETA

He does deny it.

PHORMIO

And that he knows who Stilpho was?

GETA

He does deny it.

PHORMIO

Because the poor thing was left destitute, her father is disowned; she herself is slighted: see what avarice does.

GETA [In a loud voice]

If you are going to accuse my master of avarice, you shall hear what you won't like.

DEMIPHO

Oh, the impudence of the fellow! Does he come on purpose to accuse me?

PHORMIO

For really, I have no reason why I should be offended at the young man, if he did not know him; since that person, when growing aged and poor, and supporting himself by his labor, generally confined himself to the country; there he had a piece of land from my father to cultivate; full oft, in the mean time, did the old man tell me that this kinsman of his neglected him: but what a man? The very best I ever saw in all my life.

GETA [In a loud voice]

Look to yourself as well as to him, how you speak.

PHORMIO [With affected indignation]
Away, to utter perdition, with you. For if I had not formed such an opinion of him, I should never have incurred such enmity with your family on her account, whom he now slights in such an ungenerous manner.

GETA [Aloud]
What, do you persist in speaking abusively of my master in his absence, you most abominable fellow?

PHORMIO
Why, it's just what he deserves.

GETA [Aloud]
Say you so, you jail-bird?

DEMIPHO [Calling aloud]
Geta!

GETA [Aloud]
A plunderer of people's property— a perverter of the laws!

DEMIPHO [Calling aloud]
Geta!

PHORMIO [Apart, in a low voice]
Answer him.

GETA
Who is it?
[Looking round]
Oh!—

DEMIPHO
Hold your peace.

GETA
He has never left off uttering abuse against you behind your back, unworthy of you, and just befitting himself.

DEMIPHO

Well now, have done.

[Addressing **PHORMIO**]

Young man, in the first place, with your good leave, I ask you this, if you may possibly be pleased to give me an answer: explain to me who this friend of yours was, that you speak of, and how he said that he was related to me.

PHORMIO [Sneeringly]

You are fishing it out, just as if you didn't know.

DEMIPHO

I, know?

PHORMIO

Yes.

DEMIPHO

I say I do not; you, who affirm it, recall it to my recollection.

PHORMIO

Come now, didn't you know your own cousin-german?

DEMIPHO

You torture me to death; tell me his name.

PHORMIO

His name?

DEMIPHO

Of course.

[**PHORMIO** hesitates]

Why are you silent now?

PHORMIO [Aside]

Heavens, I'm undone; I've forgot the name.

DEMIPHO

Well, what do you say?

PHORMIO [Aside, to **GETA**]

Geta, if you recollect the name I told you a short time since, prompt me.
[Aloud, to **DEMIPHO**]
Well then, I sha'n't tell you; as if you didn't know, you come to pump me.

DEMIPHO
I, come to pump you, indeed?

GETA [Whispering to **PHORMIO**]
Stilpho.

PHORMIO
But, after all, what matters that to me? It is Stilpho.

DEMIPHO
Whom did you say?

PHORMIO
Stilpho, I tell you; you knew him.

DEMIPHO
I neither know him, nor had I ever any relation of that name.

PHORMIO
Say you so? Are you not ashamed of this? But if he had left you ten talents—

DEMIPHO
May the Gods confound you!

PHORMIO
You'd have been the first, from memory, to trace your line of kindred, even as far back as from grandfather and great-grandfather.

DEMIPHO
Very likely what you say. In that case, when I had undertaken it, I should have shown how she was related to me; do you do the same: tell me, how is she related to me?

GETA
Well done, my master, that's right!

[Threateningly to **PHORMIO**]
Hark you, take you care.

PHORMIO
I've already made the matter quite plain where I ought, before the judges; besides, if it was untrue, why didn't your son disprove it?

DEMIPHO
Do you talk about my son to me? Of whose folly there is no speaking in the language it deserves.

PHORMIO
Then do you, who are so wise, go to the magistrates, that for you they may give a second decision in the same cause, since you reign alone[54] here, and are the only man allowed to get a second trial in the same cause.

DEMIPHO
Although wrong has been done me, still, however, rather than engage in litigation, or listen to you, just as though she had been my relation, as the law orders one to find her a portion, rid me of her, and take five minæ.

PHORMIO [Laughing]
Ha, ha, ha! a pleasant individual!

DEMIPHO
Well! am I asking any thing unfair? Or am I not to obtain even this, which is my right at common law?

PHORMIO
Pray, really is it so, that when you have abused her like a courtesan, the law orders you to pay her hire and pack her off? Or is it the fact, that in order that a citizen may bring no disgrace upon herself through poverty, she has been ordered to be given to her nearest relative, to pass her life with him alone? A thing which you mean to prevent.

DEMIPHO
Yes, to her nearest relative, indeed; but why to us, or on what ground?

PHORMIO

Well, well, a thing tried, they say, you can't try over again.

DEMIPHO
Not try it? On the contrary, I shall not desist until I have gone through with it.

PHORMIO
You are trifling.

DEMIPHO
Only let me alone for that.

PHORMIO
In short, Demipho, I have nothing to do with you; your son has been cast, and not you; for your time of life for marrying has now gone by.

DEMIPHO
Consider that it is he that says to you all I now say, or else assuredly, together with this wife of his, I'll be forbidding him the house.

GETA [Aside]
He's in a passion.

PHORMIO
You'll be acting more considerately.

DEMIPHO
Are you so resolved, you unlucky fellow, to do me all the mischief you can?

PHORMIO [Aside, to **GETA**]
He's afraid of us, although he's so careful to conceal it.

GETA [Aside, to **PHORMIO**]
Your beginning has turned out well.

PHORMIO
But if, on the contrary, you endure what must be endured, you'll be doing what's worthy of you, so that we may be on friendly terms.

DEMIPHO [Indignantly]

What, I seek your friendship, or have any wish to see or hear you?

PHORMIO

If you can agree with her, you will have some one to cheer up your old age; just consider your time of life.

DEMIPHO

Let her cheer up yourself; keep her to yourself.

PHORMIO

Really, do moderate your passion.

DEMIPHO

Mark what I say. There have been words enough already; if you don't make haste to fetch away the woman, I shall turn her out: I have said it, Phormio.

PHORMIO

If you use her in any other manner than is befitting a free-born woman, I shall be bringing a swinging action against you: I have said it, Demipho.
[To **GETA**]
Hark you, if there should be any occasion for me, I shall be at home.

GETA [Apart]

I understand you.

[Exit **PHORMIO**.

SCENE III

DEMIPHO, HEGIO, CRATINUS, CRITO, and **GETA.**

DEMIPHO

What care and anxiety my son does bring upon me, by entangling himself and me in this same marriage! And he doesn't so much as come into my sight, that at least I might know what he says about this matter, or what his sentiments are.

[To **GETA**]

Be off, go see whether he has returned home or not by this.

GETA

I will.

[Goes into the house.

DEMIPHO [To the **ASSISTANTS**]

You see how the case stands. What am I to do? Tell me, Hegio.

HEGIO

What, I? I think Cratinus ought, if it seems good to you.

DEMIPHO

Tell me, Cratinus.

CRATINUS

What, do you wish me to speak? I should like you to do what is most for your advantage; it is my opinion, that what this son of yours has done in your absence, in law and justice ought to be annulled; and that you'll obtain redress. That's my opinion.

DEMIPHO

Say now, Hegio.

HEGIO

I believe that he has spoken with due deliberation; but it is the fact, "as many men, so many minds;"[55] every one his own way. It doesn't appear to me that what has been done by law can be revoked; and it is wrong to attempt it.

DEMIPHO

Speak, Crito.

CRITO

I am of opinion that we must deliberate further;[56] it is a matter of importance.

HEGIO

Do you want any thing further with us?

DEMIPHO
You have done very well.

[Exeunt **ASSISTANTS**.

I am much more at a loss[57] than before.

[Re-enter **GETA**, from the house.

GETA
They say that he has not come back.

DEMIPHO
I must wait for my brother. The advice that he gives me about this matter, I shall follow. I'll go make inquiry at the harbor, when he is to come back.

[Exit.

GETA
And I'll go look for Antipho, that he may learn what has passed here. But look, I see him coming this way, just in the very nick of time.

SCENE IV

Enter **ANTIPHO**, at a distance.

ANTIPHO [To himself]
Indeed, Antipho, in many ways you are to be blamed for these feelings; to have thus run away, and intrusted your existence to the protection of other people. Did you suppose that others would give more attention to your interests than your own self? For, however other matters stood, certainly you should have thought of her whom you have now at home, that she might not suffer any harm in consequence of her confiding in you, whose hopes and resources, poor thing, are all now centred in yourself alone.

GETA [Coming forward]
Why really, master, we have for some time been censuring you here in your absence, for having thus gone away.

ANTIPHO
You are the very person I was looking for.

GETA
But still, we were not a bit the more remiss on that account.

ANTIPHO
Tell me, I beg of you, in what posture are my interests and fortunes. Has my father any suspicion?

GETA
Not any at present.

ANTIPHO
Is there still any hope?

GETA
I don't know.

ANTIPHO
Alas!

GETA
But Phædria has not neglected to use his endeavors in your behalf.

ANTIPHO
He did nothing new.

GETA
Then Phormio, too, in this matter, just as in every thing else, showed himself a man of energy.

ANTIPHO
What did he do?

GETA

With his words he silenced the old man, who was very angry.

ANTIPHO
Well done, Phormio!

GETA
I, too, did all I could.

ANTIPHO
My dear Geta, I love you all.

GETA
The commencement is just in this position, as I tell you: matters, at present, are going on smoothly, and your father intends to wait for your uncle till he arrives.

ANTIPHO
Why him?

GETA
He said he was wishful to act by his advice, in all that relates to this business.

ANTIPHO
How greatly now, Geta, I do dread my uncle's safe arrival! For, according to his single sentence, from what I hear, I am to live or die.

GETA
Here comes Phædria.

ANTIPHO
Where is he, pray?

GETA
See, he's coming from his place of exercise.[58]

SCENE V

Enter from **DORIO'S** house, **DORIO**, followed by **PHÆDRIA**.

PHÆDRIA
Prithee, hear me, Dorio.

DORIO
I'll not hear you.

PHÆDRIA
Only a moment.

DORIO
Let me alone.

PHÆDRIA
Do hear what I have to say.

DORIO
Why really I am tired of hearing the same thing a thousand times over.

PHÆDRIA
But now, I have something to tell you that you'll hear with pleasure.

DORIO
Speak then; I'm listening.

PHÆDRIA
Can I not prevail on you to wait for only three days? Whither are you going now?

DORIO
I was wondering if you had any thing new to offer.

ANTIPHO [Apart, to **GETA**]
I'm afraid for this Procurer, lest—

GETA [Apart, to **ANTIPHO**]
Something may befall his own safety.[59]

PHÆDRIA

You don't believe me?

DORIO
You guess right.

PHÆDRIA
But if I pledge my word.

DORIO
Nonsense!

PHÆDRIA
You will have reason to say that this kindness was well laid out by you on interest.

DORIO
Stuff!

PHÆDRIA
Believe me, you will be glad you did so; upon my faith, it is the truth.

DORIO
Mere dreams!

PHÆDRIA
Do but try; the time is not long.

DORIO
The same story over again.

PHÆDRIA
You will be my kinsman, my father, my friend; you—

DORIO
Now, do prate on.

PHÆDRIA
For you to be of a disposition so harsh and inexorable, that neither by pity nor by entreaties can you be softened!

DORIO

For you to be of a disposition so unreasonable and so unconscionable, Phædria, that you can be talking me over with fine words,[60] and be for amusing yourself with what's my property for nothing!

ANTIPHO [Apart, to **GETA**]

I am sorry for him.

PHÆDRIA [Aside]

Alas! I feel it to be too true.

GETA [Apart, to **ANTIPHO**]

How well each keeps up to his character!

PHÆDRIA [To himself]

And would that this misfortune had not befallen me at a time when Antipho was occupied with other cares as well.

ANTIPHO [Coming forward]

Ah Phædria, why, what is the matter?

PHÆDRIA

O most fortunate Antipho!

ANTIPHO

What, I?

PHÆDRIA

To have in your possession the object of your love, and have no occasion to encounter such a nuisance as this.

ANTIPHO

What I, in my possession? Why yes, as the saying is, I've got a wolf by the ears;[61] for I neither know how to get rid of her, nor yet how to keep her.

DORIO [Pointing to **PHÆDRIA**]

That's just my case with regard to him.

ANTIPHO [To **DORIO**]

Aye, aye, don't you show too little of the Procurer.
[To **PHÆDRIA**]
What has he been doing?

PHÆDRIA
What, he? Acting the part of a most inhuman fellow; been and sold my
Pamphila.

GETA
What! Sold her?

ANTIPHO
Sold her, say you?

PHÆDRIA
Sold her.

DORIO [Ironically]
What a shocking crime— a wench bought with one's own money!

PHÆDRIA
I can not prevail upon him to wait for me the next three days, and so far
break off the bargain with the person, while I get the money from my
friends, which has been promised me; if I don't give it him then, let him
not wait a single hour longer.

DORIO
Very good.

ANTIPHO
It's not a long time that he asks, Dorio; do let him prevail upon you; he'll
pay you two-fold for having acted to him thus obligingly.

DORIO
Mere words!

ANTIPHO
Will you allow Pamphila to be carried away from this place? And then,
besides, can you possibly allow their love to be severed asunder?

DORIO
Neither I nor you cause that.

GETA
May all the Gods grant you what you are deserving of!

DORIO
I have borne with you for several months quite against my inclination; promising and whimpering, and yet bringing nothing; now, on the other hand, I have found one to pay, and not be sniveling; give place to your betters.

ANTIPHO
I' faith, there surely was a day named, if I remember right, for you to pay him.

PHÆDRIA
It is the fact.

DORIO
Do I deny it?

ANTIPHO
Is that day past, then?

DORIO
No; but this one has come before it.

ANTIPHO
Are you not ashamed of your perfidy?

DORIO
Not at all, so long as it is for my interest.

GETA
Dunghill!

PHÆDRIA
Dorio, is it right, pray, for you to act thus?

DORIO

It is my way; if I suit you, make use of me.

ANTIPHO

Do you try to trifle with him—
[Pointing to **PHÆDRIA**]
—in this manner?

DORIO

Why really, on the contrary, Antipho, it's he trifling with me, for he knew me to be a person of this sort; I supposed him to be quite a different man; he has deceived me; I'm not a bit different to him from what I was before. But however that may be, I'll yet do this; the captain has said, that to-morrow morning he will pay me the money; if you bring it me before that, Phædria, I'll follow my rule, that he is the first served who is the first to pay. Farewell!

[Goes into his house.

SCENE VI

PHÆDRIA, ANTIPHO, and GETA.

PHÆDRIA

What am I to do? Wretch that I am! where am I now in this emergency to raise the money for him, I, who am worse than nothing? If it had been possible for these three days to be obtained of him, it was promised me by then.

ANTIPHO

Geta, shall we suffer him to continue thus wretched, when he so lately assisted me in the kind way you were mentioning? On the contrary, why not, as there's need of it, try to do him a kindness in return?

GETA

For my part, I'm sure it is but fair.

ANTIPHO

Come then, you are the only man able to serve him.

GETA
What can I do?

ANTIPHO
Procure the money.

GETA
I wish I could; but where it is to come from— tell me that.

ANTIPHO
My father has come home.

GETA
I know; but what of that?

ANTIPHO
Oh, a word to the wise[62] is quite enough.

GETA
Is that it, then?

ANTIPHO
Just so.

GETA
Upon my faith, you really do give me fine advice; out upon you! Ought I not to be heartily glad, if I meet with no mishap through your marriage, but what, in addition to that, you must now bid me, for his sake, to be seeking risk upon risk?

ANTIPHO
'Tis true what he says.

PHÆDRIΛ
What! am I a stranger to you, Geta?

GETA

I don't consider you so. But is it so trifling a matter that the old gentleman is now vexed with us all, that we must provoke him still more, and leave no room for entreaty?

PHÆDRIA
Is another man to take her away from before my eyes to some unknown spot? Alas! speak to me then, Antipho, and look upon me while you have the opportunity, and while I'm present.

ANTIPHO
Why so, or what are you going to do? Pray, tell me.

PHÆDRIA
To whatever part of the world she is borne away, I'm determined to follow her or to perish.

GETA
May the Gods prosper your design! Cautiously's the word, however.

ANTIPHO [To **GETA**]
Do see if you can give him any assistance at all.

GETA
Any at all— how?

ANTIPHO
Pray, do try, that he mayn't be doing something that we may afterward be more or less sorry for, Geta.

GETA
I'm considering.
[He pauses]
He's all safe, so far as I can guess: but still, I'm afraid of mischief.

ANTIPHO
Don't be afraid: together with you, we'll share good and bad.

GETA [To **PHÆDRIA**]
How much money do you want? Tell me.

PHÆDRIA
Only thirty minæ.

GETA
Thirty? Heyday! she's monstrous dear, Phædria.

PHÆDRIA
Indeed, she's very cheap.

GETA
Well, well, I'll get them for you.

PHÆDRIA
Oh the dear man!

[They both fall to hugging **GETA**.

GETA
Take yourselves off.

[Shakes them off.

PHÆDRIA
There's need for them directly.

GETA
You shall have them directly; but I must have Phormio for my assistant in this business.

ANTIPHO
He's quite ready; right boldly lay on him any load you like, he'll bear it: he, in especial, is a friend to his friend.

GETA
Let's go to him at once then.

ANTIPHO
Will you have any occasion for my assistance?

GETA

None; but be off home, and comfort that poor thing, who I am sure is now in-doors almost dead with fear. Do you linger?

ANTIPHO
There's nothing I could do with so much pleasure.

[Goes into the house of **DEMIPHO**.

PHÆDRIA
What way will you manage this?

GETA
I'll tell you on the road; first thing, betake yourself off.

[Exeunt

SCENE I

Enter **DEMIPHO** and **CHREMES**.

DEMIPHO
Well, have you brought your daughter with you, Chremes, for whom you went to Lemnos?

CHREMES
No.

DEMIPHO
Why not?

CHREMES
When her mother found that I staid here longer than usual, and at the same time the age of the girl did not suit with my delays, they told me that she, with all her family, set out in search of me.

DEMIPHO

Pray, then, why did you stay there so long, when you had heard of this?

CHREMES
Why, faith, a malady detained me.

DEMIPHO
From what cause? Or what was it?

CHREMES
Do you ask me? Old age itself is a malady. However, I heard that they had arrived safe, from the captain who brought them.

DEMIPHO
Have you heard, Chremes, what has happened to my son in my absence?

CHREMES
'Tis that, in fact, that has embarrassed me in my plans. For if I offer my daughter in marriage to any person that's a stranger, it must all be told how and by whom I had her. You I knew to be fully as faithful to me as I am to myself; if a stranger shall think fit to be connected with me by marriage, he will hold his tongue, just as long as good terms exist between us: but if he takes a dislike to me, he'll be knowing more than it's proper he should know. I am afraid, too, lest my wife should, by some means, come to know of it; if that is the case, it only remains for me to shake myself[63] and leave the house; for I'm the only one I can rely on at home.[64]

DEMIPHO
I know it is so, and that circumstance is a cause of anxiety to me; and I shall never cease trying, until I've made good what I promised you.

SCENE II

Enter **GETA**, on the other side of the stage, not seeing **DEMIPHO** or **CHREMES**.

GETA [To himself]

I never saw a more cunning fellow than this Phormio. I came to the fellow to tell him that money was needed, and by what means it might be procured. Hardly had I said one half, when he understood me; he was quite delighted; complimented me; asked where the old man was; gave thanks to the Gods that an opportunity was afforded him for showing himself no less a friend to Phædria than to Antipho: I bade the fellow wait for me at the Forum; whither I would bring the old gentleman. But see, here's the very man—
[Catching sight of the **OLD MAN**]
Who is the further one? Heyday, Phædria's father has got back! still, brute beast that I am, what was I afraid of? Is it because two are presented instead of one for me to dupe? I deem it preferable to enjoy a two-fold hope. I'll try for it from him from whom I first intended: if he gives it me, well and good; if I can make nothing of him, then I'll attack this newcomer.

SCENE III

Enter **ANTIPHO** from the house, behind at a distance.

ANTIPHO [To himself]
I'm expecting every moment that Geta will be here. But I see my uncle standing close by, with my father. Ah me! how much I fear what influence his return may have upon my father!

GETA [To himself]
I'll accost them.
[Goes up to them]
O welcome to you, our neighbor Chremes.

CHREMES
Save you, Geta.

GETA
I'm delighted to see you safe returned.

CHREMES
I believe you.

GETA

How go matters?

CHREMES

Many changes here upon my arrival, as usually the case.

GETA

True; have you heard what has happened to Antipho?

CHREMES

All.

GETA [To **DEMIPHO**]

What, have you told him? Disgraceful conduct, Chremes, thus to be imposed on.

DEMIPHO

It was about that I was talking to him just now.

GETA

But really, on carefully reflecting upon this matter I think I have found a remedy.

DEMIPHO

What is the remedy?

GETA

When I left you, by accident Phormio met me.

CHREMES

Who is Phormio?

GETA

He who patronized her.

CHREMES

I understand.

GETA

It seemed to me that I might first sound him; I took the fellow aside: "Phormio," said I, "why don't we try to settle these matters between us rather with a good grace than with a bad one? My master's a generous man, and one who hates litigation; but really, upon my faith, all his friends were just now advising him with one voice to turn her instantly out of doors."

ANTIPHO [Apart]
What is he about? Or where is this to end at last?

GETA [Continuing the supposed conversation]
"He'll have to give satisfaction at law, you say, if he turns her out? That has been already inquired into: aye, aye, you'll have enough to do, if you engage with him; he is so eloquent. But suppose he's beaten; still, however, it's not his life, but his money that's at stake." After I found that the fellow was influenced by these words, I said: "We are now by ourselves here; come now, what should you like to be given you, money down, to drop this suit with my master, so that she may betake herself off, and you annoy us no more?"

ANTIPHO [Apart]
Are the Gods quite on good terms with him?[65]

GETA [Continuing the conversation]
"For I'm quite sure, if you were to mention any thing that's fair and reasonable, as he is a reasonable man, you'll not have to bandy three words with him."

DEMIPHO
Who ordered you to say so?

CHREMES
Nay, he could not have more happily contrived to bring about what we want.

ANTIPHO [Apart]
Undone!

CHREMES
Go on with your story.

GETA

At first the fellow raved.

DEMIPHO

Say, what did he ask?

GETA

What? A great deal too much.

CHREMES

How much? Tell me.

GETA

Suppose he were to give a great talent.

DEMIPHO

Aye, faith, perdition to him rather; has he no shame?

GETA

Just what I said to him: "Pray," said I, "suppose he was portioning an only daughter of his own. It has been of little benefit that he hasn't one of his own, when another has been found to be demanding a fortune." To be brief, and to pass over his impertinences, this at last was his final answer: "I," said he, "from the very first, have been desirous to marry the daughter of my friend, as was fit I should; for I was aware of the ill results of this, a poor wife being married into a rich family, and becoming a slave. But, as I am now conversing with you unreservedly, I was in want of a wife to bring me a little money with which to pay off my debts; and even yet, if Demipho is willing to give as much as I am to receive with her to whom I am engaged, there is no one whom I should better like for a wife."

ANTIPHO [Apart]

Whether to say he's doing this through folly or mischief, through stupidity or design, I'm in doubt.

DEMIPHO

What if he's in debt to the amount of his life?[66]

GETA

His land is mortgaged,— for ten minæ he said.

DEMIPHO
Well, well, let him take her then; I'll give it.

GETA
He has a house besides, mortgaged for another ten.

DEMIPHO
Huy, huy! that's too much.

CHREMES
Don't be crying out; you may have those ten of me.

GETA
A lady's maid must be brought for his wife; and then too, a little more is wanted for some furniture, and some is wanted for the wedding expenses. "Well then," said he, "for these items, put down ten more."

DEMIPHO
Then let him at once bring six hundred actions[67] against me; I shall give nothing at all; is this dirty fellow to be laughing at me as well?

CHREMES
Pray do be quiet; I'll give it: do you only bring your son to marry the woman we want him to have.

ANTIPHO [Apart]
Ah me! Geta, you have ruined me by your treachery.

CHREMES
'Tis on my account she's turned off; it's right that I should bear the loss.

GETA
"Take care and let me know," said he, "as soon as possible, if they are going to let me have her, that I may get rid of the other, so that I mayn't be in doubt; for the others have agreed to pay me down the portion directly."

CHREMES

Let him have her at once; let him give notice to them that he breaks off the match with the other, and let him marry this woman.

DEMIPHO
Yes, and little joy to him of the bargain!

CHREMES
Luckily, too, I've now brought home some money with me, the rents which my wife's farms at Lemnos produce. I'll take it out of that, and tell my wife that you had occasion for it.

[They go into the house of **CHREMES**.

SCENE IV

ANTIPHO and **GETA**.

ANTIPHO [Coming forward]
Geta.

GETA
Well.

ANTIPHO
What have you been doing?

GETA
Diddling the old fellows out of their money.

ANTIPHO
Is that quite the thing?

GETA
I' faith, I don't know: it's just what I was told to do.

ANTIPHO
How now, whip-scoundrel, do you give me an answer to what I don't ask you?

[Kicks him.

GETA
What was it then that you did ask?

ANTIPHO
What was it I did ask? Through your agency, matters have most undoubtedly come to the pass that I may go hang myself. May then all the Gods, Goddesses, Deities above and below, with every evil confound you! Look now, if you wish any thing to succeed, intrust it to him who may bring you from smooth water on to a rock. What was there less advantageous than to touch upon this sore, or to name my wife? Hopes have been excited in my father that she may possibly be got rid of. Pray now, tell me, suppose Phormio receives the portion, she must be taken home by him as his wife: what's to become of me?

GETA
But he's not going to marry her.

ANTIPHO
I know that. But [ironically] when they demand the money back, of course, for our sake, he'll prefer going to prison.

GETA
There is nothing, Antipho, but what it may be made worse by being badly told: you leave out what is good, and you mention the bad. Now then, hear the other side: if he receives the money, she must be taken as his wife, you say; I grant you; still, some time at least will be allowed for preparing for the nuptials, for inviting, and for sacrificing. In the mean time, Phædria's friends will advance what they have promised; out of that he will repay it.

ANTIPHO
On what grounds? Or what will he say?

GETA
Do you ask the question? "How many circumstances, since then, have befallen me as prodigies? A strange black dog[68] entered the house; a snake came down from the tiles through the sky-light;[69] a hen

crowed;[70] the soothsayer forbade it; the diviner[71] warned me not: besides, before winter there is no sufficient reason for me to commence upon any new undertaking." This will be the case.

ANTIPHO

I only wish it may be the case.

GETA

It shall be the case; trust me for that. Your father's coming out; go tell Phædria that the money is found.

SCENE V

Enter **DEMIPHO** and **CHREMES**, from the house of the latter, the former with a purse of money.

DEMIPHO

Do be quiet, I tell you; I'll take care he shall not be playing any tricks upon us. I'll not rashly part with this without having my witnesses; I'll have it stated to whom I pay it, and for what purpose I pay it.

GETA [Apart]

How cautious he is, when there's no need for it!

CHREMES

Why yes, you had need do so, and with all haste, while the fit is upon him; for if this other woman shall prove more pressing, perhaps he may throw us over.

GETA

You've hit upon the very thing.

DEMIPHO

Lead me to him then.

GETA

I won't delay.

CHREMES [To **DEMIPHO**]

When you've done so, go over to my wife, that she may call upon her before she goes away. She must tell her that we are going to give her in marriage to Phormio, that she may not be angry with us; and that he is a fitter match for her, as knowing more of her; that we have in no way departed from our duty; that as much has been given for a portion as he asked for.

DEMIPHO

What the plague does that matter to you?

CHREMES

A great deal, Demipho. It is not enough for you to do your duty, if common report does not approve of it; I wish all this to be done with her own sanction as well, that she mayn't be saying that she has been turned out of doors.

DEMIPHO

I can do all that myself.

CHREMES

It will come better from one woman to another.

DEMIPHO

I'll ask her.

[Goes into the house of **CHREMES**; and exit **GETA**.

CHREMES [To himself]

I'm thinking where I can find them now.[72]

SCENE VI

Enter **SOPHRONA** from the house of **DEMIPHO**, at a distance.

SOPHRONA [To herself]

What am I to do? What friend, in my distress, shall I find, to whom to disclose these plans; and where shall I look for relief? For I'm afraid that my mistress, in consequence of my advice, may undeservingly sustain some injury, so extremely ill do I hear that the young man's father takes what has happened.

CHREMES [Apart, to himself]
But what old woman's this, that has come out of my brother's house, half dead with fright?

SOPHRONA [To herself, continuing]
It was distress that compelled me to this step, though I knew that the match was not likely to hold good; my object was, that in the mean time life might be supported.

CHREMES [Apart, to himself]
Upon my faith, surely, unless my recollection deceives me, or my sight's not very good, I espy my daughter's nurse.[73]

SOPHRONA [To herself]
And we are not able to find—

CHREMES [Apart]
What must I do?

SOPHRONA [To herself]
Her father.

CHREMES [To himself, apart]
Shall I accost her, or shall I wait to learn more distinctly what it is she's saying?

SOPHRONA [To herself]
If now I could find him, there's nothing that I should be in fear of.

CHREMES [Apart, to himself, aloud]
'Tis the very woman. I'll address her.

SOPHRONA [Turning round]
Who's that speaking here?

CHREMES [Coming forward]

Sophrona.

SOPHRONA
Mentioning my name, too?

CHREMES
Look round at me.

SOPHRONA [Seeing him]
Ye Gods, I do beseech you, isn't this Stilpho?

CHREMES
No.

SOPHRONA
Do you deny it?

CHREMES [In a low voice]
Step a little this way from that door, Sophrona, if you please.
[Pointing]
Don't you, henceforth, be calling me by that name.

SOPHRONA
Why? Pray, are you not the person you always used to say you were?

CHREMES [Pointing to his own house]
Hush!

SOPHRONA
Why are you afraid about that door?

CHREMES [In a low voice]
I have got a shrew of a wife shut up there. For by that name I formerly falsely called myself, in order that you might not chance indiscreetly to blab it out of doors, and then my wife, by some means or other, might come to know of it.

SOPHRONA
I' faith, that's the very reason why we, wretched creatures, have never been able to find you out here.

CHREMES
Well, but tell me, what business have you with that family from whose house you were coming out? Where are the ladies?[74]

SOPHRONA
Ah, wretched me!

CHREMES
Hah! What's the matter? Are they still alive?

SOPHRONA
Your daughter is alive. Her poor mother died of grief.

CHREMES
An unfortunate thing!

SOPHRONA
As for me, being a lone old woman, in want, and unknown, I contrived, as well as I could, to get the young woman married to the young man who is master of this house.

CHREMES
What! to Antipho?

SOPHRONA
The very same, I say.

CHREMES
What? Has he got two wives?

SOPHRONA
Dear no, prithee, he has only got this one.

CHREMES
What about the other one that's called his relative?

SOPHRONA
Why, this is she.

CHREMES

What is it you say?

SOPHRONA

It was done on purpose, in order that her lover might be enabled to marry her without a portion.

CHREMES

Ye Gods, by our trust in you! How often do those things come about through accident, which you couldn't dare to hope for? On my return, I have found my daughter matched with the very person I wished, and just as I wanted; a thing that we were both using our endeavors, with the greatest earnestness, to bring about. Without any very great management on our part, by her own management, she has by herself brought this about.

SOPHRONA

Now consider what's to be done. The young man's father has returned, and they say that he bears this with feelings highly offended.

CHREMES

There's no danger of that. But, by Gods and men, do take care that no one comes to know that she's my daughter.

SOPHRONA

No one shall know it from me.

CHREMES

Follow me; in-doors we'll hear the rest.

[He goes into **DEMIPHO'S** house, followed by **SOPHRONA**.

ACT THE FOURTH

SCENE I

Enter **DEMIPHO** and **GETA**.

DEMIPHO

'Tis caused by our own fault, that it is advantageous to be dishonest; while we wish ourselves to be styled very honest and generous. "So run away as not to run beyond the house,"[75] as the saying is. Was it not enough to receive an injury from him, but money must be voluntarily offered him as well, that he may have something on which to subsist while he plans some other piece of roguery?

GETA

Most clearly so.

DEMIPHO

They now get rewarded for it, who confound right with wrong.

GETA

Most undoubtedly.

DEMIPHO

How very foolishly, in fact, we have managed the affair with him!

GETA

If by these means we can only manage for him to marry her.

DEMIPHO

Is that, then, a matter of doubt?

GETA

I' faith, judging from what the fellow is, I don't know whether he mightn't change his mind.

DEMIPHO

How! change it indeed?

GETA

I don't know: but "if perhaps," I say.

DEMIPHO

I'll do as my brother advised me, bring hither his wife, to talk with her. Do you, Geta, go before; tell her that Nausistrata is about to visit her.

[**DEMIPHO** goes into the house of **CHREMES**.

SCENE II

GETA, alone.

GETA
The money's been got for Phædria; it's all hushed about the lawsuit; due care has been taken that she's not to leave for the present. What next, then? What's to be done? You are still sticking in the mud. You are paying by borrowing;[76] the evil that was at hand, has been put off for a day. The toils are increasing upon you, if you don't look out. Now I'll away home, and tell Phanium not to be afraid of Nausistrata, or his talking.[77]

[Goes into the house of **DEMIPHO**.

SCENE III

Enter **DEMIPHO** and **NAUSISTRATA**, from the house of **CHREMES**.

DEMIPHO
Come now, Nausistrata, after your usual way, manage to keep her in good-humor with us, and make her do of her own accord what must be done.

NAUSISTRATA
I will.

DEMIPHO
You are now seconding me with your endeavors, just as you assisted me with your money[78] before.

NAUSISTRATA
I wish to do so; and yet, i' faith, through the fault of my husband, I am less able than I ought to be.

DEMIPHO
Why so?

NAUSISTRATA
Because, i' faith, he takes such indifferent care of the property that was so industriously acquired by my father; for from those farms he used regularly to receive two talents of silver yearly; there's an instance, how superior one man is to another.

DEMIPHO
Two talents, pray?

NAUSISTRATA
Aye, and when things were much worse, two talents even.

DEMIPHO
Whew!

NAUSISTRATA
What! does this seem surprising?

DEMIPHO
Of course it does.

NAUSISTRATA
I wish I had been born a man; I'd have shown—

DEMIPHO
That I'm quite sure of.

NAUSISTRATA
In what way—

DEMIPHO
Forbear, pray, that you may be able to do battle with her; lest she, being a young woman, may be more than a match for you.

NAUSISTRATA
I'll do as you bid me; but I see my husband coming out of your house.

Enter **CHREMES**, hastily, from **DEMIPHO'S** house.

CHREMES
Ha! Demipho, has the money been paid him yet?

DEMIPHO
I took care immediately.

CHREMES
I wish it hadn't been paid him.
[On seeing **NAUSISTRATA**, aside]
Halloo, I espy my wife; I had almost said more than I ought.

DEMIPHO
Why do you wish I hadn't, Chremes?

CHREMES
It's all right.

DEMIPHO
What say you? Have you been letting her know why we are going to bring her?

[Pointing to **NAUSISTRATA**.

CHREMES
I've arranged it.

DEMIPHO
Pray, what does she say?

CHREMES
She can't be got to leave.

DEMIPHO
Why can't she?

CHREMES
Because they are fond of one another.

DEMIPHO
What's that to us?

CHREMES [Apart, to **DEMIPHO**]
A great deal; besides that, I've found out that she is related to us.

DEMIPHO [Apart]
What! You are mad, surely.

CHREMES [Apart]
So you will find; I don't speak at random; I've recovered my recollection.

DEMIPHO [Apart]
Are you quite in your senses?

CHREMES [Apart]
Nay, prithee, do take care not to injure your kinswoman.

DEMIPHO [Apart]
She is not.

CHREMES [Apart]
Don't deny it; her father went by another name; that was the cause of your mistake.

DEMIPHO [Apart]
Did she not know who was her father?

CHREMES [Apart]
She did.

DEMIPHO [Apart]
Why did she call him by another name?

CHREMES [Apart, frowning]
Will you never yield to me, nor understand what I mean?

DEMIPHO [Apart]
If you don't tell me of any thing—

CHREMES [Impatiently]
Do you persist?

NAUSISTRATA
I wonder what all this can be.

DEMIPHO
For my part, upon my faith, I don't know.

CHREMES [Whispering to him]
Would you like to know? Then, so may Jupiter preserve me, not a person is there more nearly related to her than are you and I.

DEMIPHO [Starting]
Ye Gods, by our trust in you! let's away to her; I wish for all of us, one way or other, to be sure about this.

[Going.

CHREMES [Stopping him]
Ah!

DEMIPHO
What's the matter?

CHREMES
That you should put so little confidence in me!

DEMIPHO
Do you wish me to believe you? Do you wish me to consider this as quite certain? Very well, be it so. Well, what's to be done with our friend's[79] daughter?

CHREMES
She'll do well enough.

DEMIPHO
Are we to drop her, then?

CHREMES
Why not?

DEMIPHO
The other one to stop?

CHREMES
Just so.

DEMIPHO
You may go then, Nausistrata.

NAUSISTRATA
I' faith, I think it better for all that she should remain here as it is, than as you first intended; for she seemed to me a very genteel person when I saw her.

[Goes into her house.

SCENE V

DEMIPHO and **CHREMES**.

DEMIPHO
What is the meaning of all this?

CHREMES [Looking at the door of his house]
Has she shut the door yet?

DEMIPHO
Now she has.

CHREMES
O Jupiter! the Gods do befriend us; I have found that it is my daughter married to your son.

DEMIPHO

Ha! How can that possibly be?

CHREMES

This spot is not exactly suited for me to tell it you.

DEMIPHO

Well then, step in-doors.

CHREMES

Hark you, I don't wish our sons even to come to know of this.

[They go into **DEMIPHO'S** house.

SCENE VI

Enter **ANTIPHO**.

ANTIPHO

I'm glad that, however my own affairs go, my brother has succeeded in his wishes. How wise it is to cherish desires of that nature in the mind, that when things run counter, you may easily find a cure for them! He has both got the money, and released himself from care; I, by no method, can extricate myself from these troubles; on the contrary, if the matter is concealed, I am in dread— but if disclosed, in disgrace. Neither should I now go home, were not a hope still presented me of retaining her. But where, I wonder, can I find Geta, that I may ask him what opportunity he would recommend me to take for meeting my father?

SCENE VII

Enter **PHORMIO**, at a distance.

PHORMIO [To himself]

I received the money; handed it over to the Procurer; brought away the woman, that Phædria might have her as his own— for she has now become free. Now there is one thing still remaining for me to manage,— to get a respite from the old gentlemen for carousing; for I'll enjoy myself the next few days.

ANTIPHO
But here's Phormio.
[Going up to him]
What have you to say?

PHORMIO
About what?

ANTIPHO
Why— what's Phædria going to do now? In what way does he say that he intends to take his fill of love?

PHORMIO
In his turn, he's going to act your part.

ANTIPHO
What part?

PHORMIO
To run away from his father; he begs that you in your return will act on his behalf— to plead his cause for him. For he's going to carouse at my house. I shall tell the old man that I'm going to Sunium, to the fair, to purchase the female servant that Geta mentioned a while since, so that, when they don't see me here, they mayn't suppose that I'm squandering their money. But there is a noise at the door of your house.

ANTIPHO
See who's coming out.

PHORMIO
It's Geta.

SCENE VIII

Enter **GETA**, at a distance, hastily, from the house of **DEMIPHO**.

GETA [To himself]
O fortune! O good luck![80] with blessings how great, how suddenly hast thou loaded this day with thy favors to my master Antipho!—

ANTIPHO [Apart to **PHORMIO**]
I wonder what it is he means.

GETA [Continuing]
And relieved us, his friends, from alarm; but I'm now delaying, in not throwing my cloak[81] over my shoulder—
[Throws it over his shoulder]
—and making haste to find him, that he may know what has happened.

ANTIPHO [Apart to **PHORMIO**]
Do you understand what he's talking about?

PHORMIO [Apart to **ANTIPHO**]
Do you?

ANTIPHO [Apart to **PHORMIO**]
Not at all.

PHORMIO [Apart to **ANTIPHO**]
And I just as much.

GETA [To himself]
I'll be off hence to the Procurer's; they are there just now.

[Runs along.

ANTIPHO [Calling out]
Halloo! Geta!

GETA [Still running]
There's for you. Is it any thing new or wonderful to be called back, directly you've started?

ANTIPHO
Geta!

GETA
Do you persist? Troth, you shall not on this occasion get the better of me by your annoyance.

ANTIPHO [Running after him]
Won't you stop?

GETA
You'll be getting a beating.

ANTIPHO
Assuredly that will befall yourself just now unless you stop, you whip-knave.

GETA
This must be some one pretty familiar, threatening me with a beating. [Turns round]
But is it the person I'm in search of or not? 'Tis the very man! Up to him at once.

ANTIPHO
What's the matter?

GETA
O being most blessed of all men living! For without question, Antipho, you are the only favorite of the Gods.

ANTIPHO
So I could wish; but I should like to be told why I'm to believe it is so.

GETA
Is it enough if I plunge you into a sea of joy?

ANTIPHO
You are worrying me to death.

PHORMIO
Nay but do have done with your promises, and tell us what you bring.

GETA [Looking round]
Oh, are you here too, Phormio?

PHORMIO
I am: but why do you delay?

GETA
Listen, then. When we just now paid you the money at the Forum, we went straight to Chremes; in the mean time, my master sent me to your wife.

ANTIPHO
What for?

GETA
I'll omit telling you that, as it is nothing to the present purpose, Antipho. Just as I was going to the woman's apartments, the boy Mida came running up to me, and caught me behind by my cloak, and pulled me back; I turned about, and inquired for what reason he stopped me; he said that it was forbidden for any one to go in to his mistress. "Sophrona has just now," said he, "introduced here Chremes, the old gentleman's brother," and he said that he was then in the room with them: when I heard this, on tip-toe I stole softly along; I came there, stood, held my breath, I applied my ear, and so began to listen, catching the conversation every word in this fashion.

[Shows them.

ANTIPHO
Well done, Geta.

GETA
Here I overheard a very pretty piece of business; so much so that I had nearly cried out for joy.

ANTIPHO
What was it?

GETA [Laughing]
What do you think?

ANTIPHO
I don't know.

GETA
Why, something most marvelous. Your uncle has been discovered to be the father of your wife, Phanium.

ANTIPHO [Starting]
Ha! what's that you say?

GETA
He formerly cohabited secretly with her mother at Lemnos.

PHORMIO
A dream: how could she be ignorant about her own father?

GETA
Be sure, Phormio, that there is some reason: but do you suppose that, outside of the door, I was able to understand every thing that passed between them within?

ANTIPHO
On my faith, I too have heard the same story.

GETA
Aye, and I'll give you still further reason for believing it: your uncle in the mean time came out from there; not long after he returned again, with your father; each said that he gave you permission to retain her; in fine, I've been sent to find you, and bring you to them.

ANTIPHO
Why then carry me off[82] at once;— why do you delay?

GETA
I'll do so.

ANTIPHO

O my dear Phormio, farewell!

PHORMIO

Farewell, Antipho.

[**ANTIPHO** and **GETA** go into **DEMIPHO'S** house.

PHORMIO, alone.

PHORMIO

So may the Gods bless me, this has turned out luckily. I'm glad of it, that such good fortune has thus suddenly befallen them. I have now an excellent opportunity for diddling the old men, and ridding Phædria of all anxiety about the money, so that he mayn't be under the necessity of applying to any of his companions. For this same money, as it has been given him, shall be given for good, whether they like it or not: how to force them to this, I've found out the very way. I must now assume a new air and countenance. But I'll betake myself off to this next alley; from that spot I'll present myself to them, when they come out of doors. I sha'n't go to the fair, where I pretended I was going.

[He retires into the alley.

ACT THE FIFTH

SCENE I

Enter **DEMIPHO** and **CHREMES**, from **DEMIPHO'S** house.

DEMIPHO

I do give and return hearty thanks to the Gods, and with reason, brother, inasmuch as these matters have turned out for us so fortunately. We must now meet with Phormio as soon as possible, before he squanders our thirty minæ, so that we may get them from him.

[Enter **PHORMIO**, coming forward, and speaking aloud, as though not seeing them.

PHORMIO
I'll go see if Demipho's at home; that as to what[83]—

DEMIPHO [Accosting him]
Why, Phormio, we were coming to you.

PHORMIO
Perhaps about the very same affair.

[**DEMIPHO** nods assent.

I' faith, I thought so. What were you coming to my house for? Ridiculous; are you afraid that I sha'n't do what I have once undertaken? Hark you, whatever is my poverty, still, of this one thing I have taken due care, not to forfeit my word.

CHREMES [To **DEMIPHO**]
Is she not genteel-looking,[84] just as I told you?

DEMIPHO
Very much so.

PHORMIO
And this is what I'm come to tell you, Demipho, that I'm quite ready; whenever you please, give me my wife. For I postponed all my other business, as was fit I should, when I understood that you were so very desirous to have it so.

DEMIPHO [Pointing to **CHREMES**]
But he has dissuaded me from giving her to you. "For what," says he, "will be the talk among people if you do this? Formerly, when she might have been handsomely disposed of, then she wasn't given; now it's a disgrace for her to be turned out of doors, a repudiated woman;" pretty nearly, in

fact, all the reasons which you yourself, some little time since, were urging to me.

PHORMIO
Upon my faith, you are treating me in a very insulting manner.

DEMIPHO
How so?

PHORMIO
Do you ask me? Because I shall not be able to marry the other person I mentioned; for with what face shall I return to her whom I've slighted?

CHREMES
Then besides, I see that Antipho is unwilling to part with her.
[Aside, prompting **DEMIPHO**]
Say so.

DEMIPHO
Then besides, I see that my son is very unwilling to part with the damsel. But have the goodness to step over to the Forum, and order this money to be transferred to my account,[85] Phormio.

PHORMIO
What, when I've paid it over to the persons to whom I was indebted?

DEMIPHO
What's to be done, then?

PHORMIO
If you will let me have her for a wife, as you promised, I'll take her; but if you prefer that she should stay with you, the portion must stay with me, Demipho. For it isn't fair that I should be misled for you, as it was for your own sakes that I broke off with the other woman, who was to have brought me a portion just as large.

DEMIPHO
Away with you to utter perdition, with this swaggering, you vagabond. What, then, do you fancy we don't know you, or your doings?

PHORMIO
You are provoking me.

DEMIPHO
Would you have married her, if she had been given to you?

PHORMIO
Try the experiment.

DEMIPHO
That my son might cohabit with her at your house, that was your design.

PHORMIO
Pray, what is that you say?

DEMIPHO
Then do you give me my money?

PHORMIO
Nay, but do you give me my wife?

DEMIPHO
Come before a magistrate.

[Going to seize hold of him.

PHORMIO
Why, really, if you persist in being troublesome—

DEMIPHO
What will you do?

PHORMIO
What, I? You fancy, perhaps, just now, that I am the protector of the portionless; for the well portioned,[86] I'm in the habit of being so as well.

CHREMES
What's that to us?

PHORMIO [With a careless air]

Nothing at all. I know a certain lady here—
[Pointing at **CHREMES'S** house]
—whose husband had—

CHREMES [Starting]
Ha!

DEMIPHO
What's the matter?

PHORMIO
Another wife at Lemnos—

CHREMES [Aside]
I'm ruined!

PHORMIO
By whom he had a daughter; and her he is secretly bringing up.

CHREMES [Aside]
I'm dead and buried!

PHORMIO
This I shall assuredly now inform her of.

[Walks toward the house.

CHREMES [Running and catching hold of him]
I beg of you, don't do so.

PHORMIO [With a careless air]
Oh, were you the person?

DEMIPHO
What a jest he's making of us.

CHREMES [To **PHORMIO**]
We'll let you off.

PHORMIO

Nonsense.

CHREMES
What would you have? We'll forgive you the money you've got.

PHORMIO
I hear you. Why the plague, then, do you two trifle with me in this way, you silly men, with your childish speeches—"I won't, and I will; I will, and I won't," over again: "keep it, give it me back; what has been said, is unsaid; what had been just a bargain, is now no bargain."

CHREMES [Aside, to **DEMIPHO**]
In what manner, or from whom has he come to know of this?

DEMIPHO [Aside]
I don't know; but that I've told it to no one, I know for certain.

CHREMES [Aside]
So may the Gods bless me, 'tis as good as a miracle.

PHORMIO [Aside, to himself]
I've graveled them.

DEMIPHO [Apart, to **CHREMES**]
Well now, is he to be carrying off[87] from us such a sum of money as this, and so palpably to impose upon us? By heavens, I'd sooner die. Manage to show yourself of resolute and ready wit. You see that this slip of yours has got abroad, and that you can not now possibly conceal it from your wife; it is then more conducive to our quiet, Chremes, ourselves to disclose what she will be hearing from others; and then, in our own fashion, we shall be able to take vengeance upon this dirty fellow.

PHORMIO [Aside, to himself]
Good lack-a-day, now's the sticking-point, if I don't look out for myself. They are making toward me with a gladiatorial air.

CHREMES [Apart, to **DEMIPHO**]
But I doubt whether it's possible for her to be appeased.

DEMIPHO [Apart, to **CHREMES**]
Be of good courage; I'll effect a reconciliation between you; remembering this, Chremes, that she is dead[88] and gone by whom you had this girl.

PHORMIO [In a loud voice]
Is this the way you are going to deal with me? Very cleverly done. Come on with you. By heavens, Demipho, you have provoked me, not to his advantage.
[Pointing at **CHREMES**]
How say you?
[Addressing **CHREMES**]
When you've been doing abroad just as you pleased, and have had no regard for this excellent lady here, but on the contrary, have been injuring her in an unheard-of manner, would you be coming to me with prayers to wash away your offenses? On telling her of this, I'll make her so incensed with you, that you sha'n't quench her, though you should melt away into tears.

DEMIPHO [Aside]
A plague may all the Gods and Goddesses send upon him. That any fellow should be possessed of so much impudence! Does not this villain deserve to be transported hence to some desolate land at the public charge?

CHREMES [Aside]
I am brought to such a pass, that I really don't know what to do in it.

DEMIPHO
I know; let's go into court.

PHORMIO
Into court? Here in preference—
[Pointing to **CHREMES'S** house]
—if it suits you in any way.

[Moves toward the house.

DEMIPHO [To **CHREMES**]
Follow him, and hold him back, till I call out the servants.

CHREMES [Trying to seize **PHORMIO**]

But I can't by myself; run and help me.

PHORMIO [To **DEMIPHO**, who seizes hold of him]
There's one action of damages against you.

CHREMES
Sue him at law, then.

PHORMIO
And another with you, Chremes.

DEMIPHO
Lay hold of him.

[They both drag him.

PHORMIO
Is it thus you do? Why then I must exert my voice:
[Calling aloud]
Nausistrata, come out

CHREMES [To **DEMIPHO**]
Stop his mouth.

DEMIPHO
See how strong the rascal is.

PHORMIO [Calling aloud]
Nausistrata, I say.

CHREMES
Will you not hold your tongue?

PHORMIO
Hold my tongue?

DEMIPHO [To **CHREMES**, as they drag him along]
If he won't follow, plant your fists in his stomach.

PHORMIO

Or e'en gouge out an eye. The time's coming when I shall have a full revenge on you.

Enter **NAUSISTRATA**, in haste, from the house.

NAUSISTRATA
Who calls my name?

CHREMES [In alarm]
Ha!

NAUSISTRATA
My husband, pray what means this disturbance?

PHORMIO [To **CHREMES**]
Oh, oh, why are you mute now?

NAUSISTRATA
Who is this man? Won't you answer me?

PHORMIO
What, he to answer you? who, upon my faith, doesn't know where he is.

CHREMES [To **NAUSISTRATA**]
Take care how you believe that fellow in any thing.

PHORMIO [To **NAUSISTRATA**]
Go, touch him; if he isn't in a cold sweat all over, why then kill me.

CHREMES
'Tis nothing at all.

NAUSISTRATA
What is it, then, that this person is talking about?

PHORMIO

You shall know directly; listen now.

CHREMES
Are you resolved to believe him?

NAUSISTRATA
Pray, how can I believe him, when he has told me nothing?

PHORMIO
The poor creature is distracted from fright.

NAUSISTRATA
It isn't for nothing, i' faith, that you are in such a fright.

CHREMES
What, I in a fright?

PHORMIO [To **CHREMES**]
All right, of course: since you are not in a fright at all, and this is nothing at all that I'm going to tell, do you relate it.

DEMIPHO
Villain, is he to relate it at your request?

PHORMIO [To **DEMIPHO**]
Come now, you've managed nicely for your brother.

NAUSISTRATA
My husband, will you not tell me?

CHREMES
But—

NAUSISTRATA
But what?

CHREMES
There's no need to tell you.

PHORMIO

Not for you, indeed; but there's need for her to know it. At Lemnos—

CHREMES [Starting]
Ha! what are you doing?

DEMIPHO [To **PHORMIO**]
Won't you hold your tongue?

PHORMIO [To **NAUSISTRATA**]
Unknown to you—

CHREMES
Ah me!

PHORMIO
He married another—

NAUSISTRATA
My dear sir, may the Gods forbid it!

PHORMIO
Such is the fact.

NAUSISTRATA
Wretch that I am, I'm undone!

PHORMIO
And had a daughter by her, too, while you never dreamed of it.

CHREMES
What are we to do?

NAUSISTRATA
O immortal Gods!—a disgraceful and a wicked misdeed!

DEMIPHO [Aside, to **CHREMES**]
It's all up with you.

PHORMIO

Was ever any thing now more ungenerously done? Your men, who, when they come to their wives, then become incapacitated from old age.

NAUSISTRATA
Demipho, I appeal to you; for with that man it is irksome for me to speak. Were these those frequent journeys and long visits at Lemnos? Was this the lowness of prices that reduced our rents?

DEMIPHO
Nausistrata, I don't deny that in this matter he has been deserving of censure; but still, it may be pardoned.

PHORMIO [Apart]
He is talking to the dead.

DEMIPHO
For he did this neither through neglect or aversion to yourself. About fifteen years since, in a drunken fit, he had an intrigue with this poor woman, of whom this girl was born, nor did he ever touch her afterward. She is dead and gone: the only difficulty that remained in this matter. Wherefore, I do beg of you, that, as in other things, you'll bear this with patience.

NAUSISTRATA
Why should I with patience? I could wish, afflicted as I am, that there were an end now of this matter. But how can I hope? Am I to suppose that, at his age, he will not offend in future? Was he not an old man then, if old age makes people behave themselves decently? Are my looks and my age more attractive now, Demipho? What do you advance to me, to make me expect or hope that this will not happen any more?

PHORMIO [In a loud voice]
Those who have[89] a mind to come to the funeral of Chremes, why now's their time. 'Tis thus I retaliate: come now, let him challenge Phormio who pleases: I'll have him victimized[90] with just a like mischance. Why then, let him return again into her good graces. I have now had revenge enough. She has got something for her as long as she lives, to be forever ringing into his ears.

NAUSISTRATA

But it was because I deserved this, I suppose; why should I now, Demipho, make mention of each particular, how I have conducted myself toward him?

DEMIPHO
I know it all, as well as yourself.

NAUSISTRATA
Does it appear, then, that I deserved this treatment?

DEMIPHO
Far from it: but since, by reproaching, it can not now be undone, forgive him: he entreats you—he begs your pardon—owns his fault—makes an apology. What would you have more?

PHORMIO [Aside]
But really, before she grants pardon to him, I must take care of myself and Phædria.
[To **NAUSISTRATA**]
Hark you, Nausistrata, before you answer him without thinking, listen to me.

NAUSISTRATA
What's the matter?

PHORMIO
I got out of him thirty minæ by a stratagem. I give them to your son; he paid them to a Procurer for his mistress.

CHREMES
Ha! what is it you say?

PHORMIO [Sneeringly]
Does it seem to you so very improper for your son, a young man, to keep one mistress, while you have two wives? Are you ashamed of nothing? With what face will you censure him? Answer me that.

DEMIPHO
He shall do as you wish.

NAUSISTRATA

Nay, that you may now know my determination. I neither forgive nor promise any thing, nor give any answer, before I see my son: to his decision I leave every thing. What he bids me, I shall do.

DEMIPHO

You are a wise woman, Nausistrata.

NAUSISTRATA

Does that satisfy you, Chremes?

CHREMES

Yes, indeed, I come off well, and fully to my satisfaction; indeed, beyond my expectation.

NAUSISTRATA [To **PHORMIO**]

Do you tell me, what is your name?

PHORMIO

What, mine? Phormio; a well-wisher to your family, upon my honor, and to your son Phaedria in particular.

NAUSISTRATA

Then, Phormio, on my word, henceforward I'll both do and say for you all I can, and whatever you may desire.

PHORMIO

You speak obligingly.

NAUSISTRATA

I' faith, it is as you deserve.

PHORMIO

First, then, will you do this, Nausistrata, at once, to please me, and to make your husband's eyes ache with vexation?

NAUSISTRATA

With all my heart.

PHORMIO

Invite me to dinner.

NAUSISTRATA
Assuredly indeed, I do invite you.

DEMIPHO
Let us now away in-doors.

CHREMES
By all means; but where is Phaedria, our arbitrator?

PHORMIO
I'll have him here just now.
[To the **AUDIENCE**]
Fare you well, and grant us your applause.[91]

ADDITIONAL SCENE

[Which is generally considered to be spurious]

Enter **PHÆDRIA** and **PHORMIO**, from opposite sides of the stage.

PHÆDRIA
Assuredly there is a God, who both hears and sees what we do. And I do not consider that to be true which is commonly said: "Fortune frames and fashions the affairs of mankind, just as she pleases."

PHORMIO [Aside]
Heyday! what means this? I've met with Socrates, not Phædria, so far as I see. Why hesitate to go up and address him?
[Accosting him]
How now, Phædria, whence have you acquired this new wisdom, and derived such great delight, as you show by your countenance?

PHÆDRIA
O welcome, my friend; O most delightful Phormio, welcome! There's not a person in all the world I could more wish just now to meet than yourself.

PHORMIO
Pray, tell me what is the matter.

PHÆDRIA
Aye, faith, I have to beg of you, that you will listen to it. My Pamphila is a citizen of Attica, and of noble birth, and rich.

PHORMIO
What is it you tell me? Are you dreaming, pray?

PHÆDRIA
Upon my faith, I'm saying what's true.

PHORMIO
Yes, and this, too, is a true saying: "You'll have no great difficulty in believing that to be true, which you greatly wish to be so."

PHÆDRIA
Nay, but do listen, I beg of you, to all the wonderful things I have to tell you of. It was while thinking of this to myself, that I just now burst forth into those expressions which you heard—that we, and what relates to us, are ruled by the sanction of the Gods, and not by blind chance.

PHORMIO
I've been for some time in a state of suspense.

PHÆDRIA
Do you know Phanocrates?

PHORMIO
As well as I do yourself.

PHÆDRIA
The rich man?

PHORMIO
I understand.

PHÆDRIA

He is the father of Pamphila. Not to detain you, these were the circumstances: Calchas was his servant, a worthless, wicked fellow. Intending to run away from the house, he carried off this girl, whom her father was bringing up in the country, then five years old, and, secretly taking her with him to Eubæa, sold her to Lycus, a merchant. This person, a long time after, sold her, when now grown up, to Dorio. She, however, knew that she was the daughter of parents of rank, inasmuch as she recollected herself being attended and trained up by female servants: the name of her parents she didn't recollect.

PHORMIO
How, then, were they discovered?

PHÆDRIA
Stay; I was coming to that. This runaway was caught yesterday, and sent back to Phanocrates: he related the wonderful circumstances I have mentioned about the girl, and how she was sold to Lycus, and afterward to Dorio. Phanocrates sent immediately, and claimed his daughter; but when he learned that she had been sold, he came running to me.

PHORMIO
O, how extremely fortunate!

PHÆDRIA
Phanocrates has no objection to my marrying her; nor has my father, I imagine.

PHORMIO
Trust me for that; I'll have all this matter managed for you; Phormio has so arranged it, that you shall not be a suppliant to your father, but his judge.

PHÆDRIA
You are joking.

PHORMIO
So it is, I tell you. Do you only give me the thirty minæ which Dorio—

PHÆDRIA

You put me well in mind; I understand you; you may have them; for he must give them back, as the law forbids a free woman to be sold; and, on my faith, I do rejoice that an opportunity is afforded me of rewarding you, and taking a hearty vengeance upon him; a monster of a fellow! he has feelings more hardened than iron.

PHORMIO

Now, Phædria, I return you thanks; I'll make you a return upon occasion, if ever I have the opportunity. You impose a heavy task upon me, to be contending with you in good offices, as I can not in wealth; and in affection and zeal, I must repay you what I owe. To be surpassed in deserving well, is a disgrace to a man of principle.

PHÆDRIA

Services badly bestowed, I take to be disservices. But I do not know any person more grateful and more mindful of a service than yourself. What is it you were just now mentioning about my father?

PHORMIO

There are many particulars, which at present I have not the opportunity to relate. Let's go in-doors, for Nausistrata has invited me to dinner, and I'm afraid we may keep them waiting.

PHÆDRIA

Very well; follow me.
[To the **AUDIENCE**]
Fare you well, and grant us your applause.

FOOTNOTES

[Footnote 1: From δημὸς, "the people," and φῶς "light".]

[Footnote 2: See the Dramatis Personæ of the Andria.]

[Footnote 3: See the Dramatis Personæ of the Eunuchus.]

[Footnote 4: See the Dramatis Personæ of the Eunuchus.]

[Footnote 5: From φορμὸς, "an osier basket."]

[Footnote 6: See the Dramatis Personæ of the Adelphi.]

[Footnote 7: See the Dramatis Personæ of the Andria.]

[Footnote 8: See the Dramatis Personæ of the Adelphi.]

[Footnote 9: From κρατὸς, "strength."]

[Footnote 10: See the Dramatis Personæ of the Andria.]

[Footnote 11: From Doris, his country, a part of Caria.]

[Footnote 12: From ναῦς, "a ship," and στρατὸς, "an army."]

[Footnote 13: See the Dramatis Personæ of the Eunuchus.]

[Footnote 14: The Roman Games]—The "ludi Romani," or "Roman Games," were first established by Ancus Marcius, and were celebrated in the month of September.]

[Footnote 15: Four times]—The numerals signifying "four," Donatus takes to mean that this was the fourth Play composed by Terence; it is, however, more generally supposed that the meaning is, that it was acted four times in one year.]

[Footnote 16: Being Consuls]—M. Valerius Messala and C. Fannius Strabo were Consuls in the year from the Building of the City 591, and B.C. 162.]

[Footnote 17: Since the old Poet]—Ver. 1. He alludes to his old enemy, Luscus Lavinius, who is mentioned in all his Prologues, except those to the Hecyra.]

[Footnote 18: While one implored]—Ver. 8. "Et eam plorare, orare ut subveniat sibi." This is probably in allusion to some absurd passage in one of the Plays of Lavinius. It is generally supposed to mean, that the stag implores the young man; but as the youth is mad, the absurdity, of the passage is heightened if we suppose that he implores the stag, and, in the moment of its own danger, entreats it to come to his own assistance; as certainly the Latin will admit of that interpretation.—Ovid has a somewhat similar passage in the Pontic Epistles, B. ii. Ep. ii. l. 39: "The hind that, in its terror, is flying from the savage dogs, hesitates not to trust itself to the neighboring house."]

[Footnote 19: Epidicazomenos]—Ver. 25. A Play of Apollodorus, so called from that Greek word, signifying "one who demands justice from another," in allusion to Phormio, who is the complainant in the suit, which is the foundation of the plot.]

[Footnote 20: Was driven from the place]—Ver. 32. Alluding, probably, to the disturbances which took place at the first representation of the Hecyra, and which are mentioned in the Prologues to that Play.]

[Footnote 21: Davus]—Davus is a protatic character, only introduced for the purpose of opening the story.]

[Footnote 22: Out of his allowance]—Ver. 43. Donatus tells us that the slaves received four "modii," or measures of corn, each month, which was called their "demensum."]

[Footnote 23: Will be struck]—Ver. 48. "Ferietur." "To strike" a person for a present was said when it was extorted from him reluctantly. So in the Trinummus of Plautus, l. 247, "Ibi illa pendentem ferit." "Then does she strike while he is wavering."]

[Footnote 24: For another present]—Ver. 48. Presents were usually made to persons on their birthday, on the day of their marriage, and on the birth of their children.]

[Footnote 25: Initiate him]—Ver. 49. It is not known what initiation is here referred to. Madame Dacier thinks it was an initiation into the great mysteries of Ceres, which was commonly performed while children were yet very young; others suggest that it means the period of weaning the child, and initiating it into the use of another kind of diet. Donatus says, that Varro speaks of children being initiated into the mysteries of the

Deities Edulia, Potica, and Cuba, the Divinities of Eating, Drinking, and Sleeping.]

[Footnote 26: Ready counted out]—Ver. 53. "Lectum," literally "picked out" or "chosen"—the coins being of full weight.]

[Footnote 27: Have been angry with me]—Ver. 74. He alludes to the common belief that each person had a Genius or Guardian Deity; and that when misfortune overtook him, he had been abandoned by his Genius.]

[Footnote 28: Kick against the spur]—Ver. 78. "To kick against the pricks," or "in spite of the spur," was a common Greek proverb. The expression occurs in the New Testament, Acts ix. 5. "It is hard for thee to kick against the pricks."]

[Footnote 29: To make your market]—Ver. 79. This is a metaphorical expression taken from traffic, in which merchants suit themselves to the times, and fix a price on their commodities, according to the course of the market.]

[Footnote 30: To the school]—Ver. 86. It was the custom for the "lenones," or "procurers," to send their female slaves to music-schools, in order to learn accomplishments. So in the Prologue to the Rudens of Plautus: "This Procurer brought the maiden to Cyrene hither. A certain Athenian youth, a citizen of this city, beheld her us she was going home from the music-school."]

[Footnote 31: Young man in tears]—Ver. 92. In the Play of Apollodorus, it was the barber himself that gave the account how he had just returned from cutting off the young woman's hair, which was one of the usual ceremonies in mourning among the Greeks. Donatus remarks, that Terence altered this circumstance that he might not shock a Roman audience by a reference to manners so different from their own.]

[Footnote 32: Take out a summons]—Ver. 127. "Dica" was the writ or summons with which an action at law was commenced.]

[Footnote 33: Usher to the Music-girl]—Ver. 144. This is said satirically of Phaedria, who was in the habit of escorting the girl to the music-school. It was the duty of the "pædagogi," or "tutors," to lead the children to school,

who were placed under their care. See the speech of Lydus, the
pædagogus of Pistoclerus, in the Bacchides of Plautus, Act iii. Sc. 3, where,
enlarging upon his duties, he mentions this among them.]

[Footnote 34: Sever from me this connection]—Ver. 161. By forcing him to
divorce her.]

[Footnote 35: Neither right]—Ver. 176. No right to get rid of her in
consequence of the judgment which, at the suit of Phormio, has been
pronounced against him; nor yet, right to keep her, because of his father
insisting upon turning her out of doors.]

[Footnote 36: Be washing a brickbat]—Ver. 187. "Laterem lavare," "to
wash a brick," or "tile," was a proverb signifying labor in vain, probably
because (if the brick was previously baked) it was impossible to wash
away the red color of it. According to some, the saying alluded to the act
of washing a brick which had been only dried in the sun, in which case the
party so doing both washed away the brick and soiled his own fingers.]

[Footnote 37: Here in reserve]—Ver. 230. "Succenturiatus." The
"succenturiati" were, properly, men intrusted to fill up vacancies in the
centuries or companies, when thinned by battle.]

[Footnote 38: Let alone "authority"]—Ver. 232. "Ac mitto imperium."
Cicero has quoted this passage in his Epistles to Atticus, B. ii. Ep. 19.]

[Footnote 39: When affairs are the most prosperous]—Ver. 241. Cicero
quotes this passage in the Third Book of his Tusculan Questions, and the
maxim here inculcated was a favorite one with the Stoic philosophers.]

[Footnote 40: Any giving evidence]—Ver. 293. Slaves were neither allowed
to plead for themselves, nor to give evidence. See the Curculio of Plautus,
l. 621, and the Notes to the Andria.]

[Footnote 41: Given her a portion]—Ver. 297. By this remark, Donatus
observes that Terence artfully prepares us for the imposition of Phormio,
who extorts money from the old gentleman on this very ground.]

[Footnote 42: While you were living]—Ver. 302. There was a law at Athens
which enacted that persons who lent money to young men in the lifetime

of their parents should have no power to recover it. In line 303 of the Pseudolus, Plautus alludes to the Quinavicenarian or Lætorian Law, at Rome, which forbade credit to be given to persons under the age of twenty-five years, and deprived the creditor of all right to recover his money or goods.]

[Footnote 43: The woman's next friend]—Ver. 307. The "patronus" was the person who undertook to conduct a lawsuit for another.]

[Footnote 44: Salute the household Gods]—Ver. 311. It was the custom for those returning from a voyage or journey, to give thanks to their household Gods for having protected them in their absence. Thus, in the Amphitryon of Plautus, Jupiter, while personating Amphitryon, pretends, in l. 983, that he is going to offer sacrifice for his safe return.]

[Footnote 45: And so you say]—Ver. 315. Donatus tells the following story with reference to this passage: "This Play being once rehearsed before Terence and some of his most intimate acquaintances, Ambivius, who acted the part of Phormio, came in drunk, which threw the author into a violent passion; but Ambivius had scarcely repeated a few lines, stammering and scratching his head, before Terence became pacified, declaring that when he was writing these very lines, he had exactly such a Parasite as Ambivius then represented, in his thoughts."]

[Footnote 46: Have hashed it up]—Ver. 318. He is thought to allude here, figuratively, to the composition of a dish called "moretum," (in praise of which Virgil wrote a poem) which was composed of garlic, onions, cheese, eggs, and other ingredients, beaten up in a mortar. The allusion to eating is appropriately used in an address to a Parasite.]

[Footnote 47: Turn upon myself]—Ver. 323. Donatus observes that in this Scene Terence exhibits the lower order of Parasites, who ingratiated themselves by sharping and roguery, as in the Eunuchus he describes Parasites of a higher rank, and of a newer species, who obtained their ends by flattery.]

[Footnote 48: In the stocks at last]—Ver. 325. "In nervum crumpat denique." There are several interpretations suggested for these words. Some think they allude to the drawing of a bow till it breaks; but they are more generally thought to imply termination in corporal punishment.

"Nervus" is supposed to have been the name of a kind of stocks used in torturing slaves, and so called from being formed, in part at least, of the sinews of animals.]

[Footnote 49: They will take you]—Ver. 334. At Rome, insolvent debtors became the slaves of their creditors till their debts were paid.]

[Footnote 50: To his patron]—Ver. 338. "Regi." The Parasites were in the habit of calling their patron "Rex," their "King."]

[Footnote 51: At free cost]—Ver. 339. "Asymbolum." Without having paid his "symbola," or "club," for the entertainment. Donatus informs us that the whole of this passage is borrowed from one of Ennius, which is still preserved.]

[Footnote 52: First to drink]—Ver. 342. To be the first to drink, and to take the higher place on the couch when eating, was the privilege of the most honored guests, who usually bathed, and were then anointed before the repast.]

[Footnote 53: Banquet full of doubts]—Ver. 342. "Coena dubia." Horace, who borrows many of his phrases from Terence, uses the same expression.]

[Footnote 54: Since you reign alone]—Ver. 605. This is a remark well put into the mouth of an Athenian, as the public were very jealous of any person becoming paramount to the laws, and to prevent it, were frequently guilty of the most odious oppression.]

[Footnote 55: So many minds]—Ver. 454. "Quot homines, tot sententiæ." This is a famous adage. One similar to the succeeding one is found in the Second Eclogue of Virgil, l. 65: "Trahit sua quemque voluptas," exactly equivalent to our saying, "Every man to his taste."]

[Footnote 56: Must deliberate further]—Ver. 457. "Amplius deliberandum." This is probably a satirical allusion to the judicial system of procrastination, which, by the Romans, was called "ampliatio." When the judges could not come to a satisfactory conclusion about a cause, they signified it by the letters N. L. (for "non liquet," "it is not clear"), and put off the suit for a rehearing.]

[Footnote 57: Much more at a loss]—Ver. 459. See the Poenulus of Plautus, where advocates or assistants are introduced among the Dramatic Personæ. Colman has the following remarks on this quaint passage: "I believe there is no Scene in Comedy more highly seasoned with the ridiculous than this before us. The idea is truly comic, and it is worked up with all that simplicity and chastity so peculiar to the manner of Terence. An ordinary writer would have indulged himself in twenty little conceits on this occasion; but the dry gravity of Terence infinitely surpasses, as true humor, all the drolleries which, perhaps, even those great masters of Comedy, Plautus or Molière, might have been tempted to throw out. It is the highest art of a Dramatic Author, on some occasions, to leave a good deal to the Actor; and it has been remarked by Heinsius and others, that Terence was particularly attentive to this circumstance."]

[Footnote 58: From his place of exercise]—Ver. 484. "Palæstra." He alludes to the Procurer's house under this name.]

[Footnote 59: Befall his own safety]—Ver. 490. Overhearing Phædria earnest and determined, and the Procurer obstinate and inflexible, Antipho and Geta join in apprehending that the brutality of the latter may provoke Phædria to some act of violence.]

[Footnote 60: With fine words]—Ver. 499. "Phaleratis dictis." "Phaleræ" were, properly, the silver ornaments with which horses were decked out, and being only for show, and not for use, gave rise to this saying. "Ductes" was an obscene word, and not likely to be used by any but such characters as Dorio.]

[Footnote 61: A wolf by the ears]—Ver. 505. A proverbial expression which, according to Suetonius, was frequently in the mouth of Tiberius Cæsar.]

[Footnote 62: A word to the wise]—Ver. 540. "Dictum sapienti sat est." The same proverb is found in the Persa of Plautus, l. 736.]

[Footnote 63: To shake myself]—Ver. 585. "Me excutiam." In reference to the custom of the Greeks, and the Eastern nations, of shaking their clothes at the door of any house which they were going to leave.]

[Footnote 64: Rely on at home]—Ver. 586. "Nam ego meorum solus sum meus." He means that he is the only person in his house friendly to himself, inasmuch as his wife, from her wealth, has supreme power over the domestics, in whom he himself can place no trust.]

[Footnote 65: Good terms with him]—Ver. 635. Meaning, "Is he in his senses or not?"]

[Footnote 66: Amount of his life]—Ver. 660. "Quid si animam debet?" Erasmus tells us that this was a proverb among the Greeks applied to those who ran so deeply in debt, that their persons, and consequently, in one sense, their very existence, came into the power of their creditors.]

[Footnote 67: Six hundred actions]—Ver. 667. "Sescentos;" literally, "six hundred." The Romans used this term as we do the words "ten thousand," to signify a large, but indefinite number.]

[Footnote 68: A strange black dog]—Ver. 705. This omen, Plautus calls, in the Casina, l. 937, "canina scæva."]

[Footnote 69: Through the sky-light]—Ver. 706. So in the Amphitryon of Plautus, l. 1108, two great snakes come down through the "impluvium," or "sky-light." On the subject of the "impluvium," see the Notes to the Miles Gloriosus of Plautus, l. 159.]

[Footnote 70: A hen crowed]—Ver. 707. Donatus tells us that it was a saying, that in the house where a hen crowed, the wife had the upper hand.]

[Footnote 71: The soothsayer—the diviner]—Ver. 708. According to some accounts there was this difference between the "hariolus" and the "aruspex," that the former foretold human events, the latter those relating to the Deities. Donatus has remarked on these passages, that Terence seems to sneer at the superstitions referred to.]

[Footnote 72: Can find them now]—Ver. 726. His Lemnian wife and daughter. Colman remarks: "This is intended as a transition to the next Scene; but I think it would have been better if it had followed without this kind of introduction. The Scene itself is admirable, and is, in many places, both affecting and comic, and the discovery of the real character of Phanium is made at a very proper time."]

[Footnote 73: My daughter's nurse]—Ver. 735. Among the ancients, it was the custom for nurses who had brought up children to remain with them in after-life.]

[Footnote 74: Where are the ladies?]—Ver. 748. "Ubi illæ?" literally, "Where are these women?"]

[Footnote 75: Run beyond the house]—Ver. 767. "Fugias ne præter casam." This passage has given much trouble to the Commentators; but it is pretty clear that the explanation of Donatus is the correct one: "Don't abandon your own home," that being the safest place. Stallbaum agrees with Gronovius in thinking that it was first applied as a piece of advice to runaway slaves, as being likely to become worse off by the change; probably much in the same spirit as we say, "Out of the frying-pan into the fire."]

[Footnote 76: Paying by borrowing]—Ver. 779. "Versura solvere," was "to pay a debt by borrowing money," and consequently to be no better off than before. Geta having, by the money he has procured, freed Phædria from all danger of losing his mistress, but at the same time having brought Antipho into still greater danger of losing his wife.]

[Footnote 77: Or his talking]—Ver. 782. "Ejus" here alludes, not to Nausistrata but to Phormio. Madame Dacier suggests that it should be "hujus."]

[Footnote 78: With your money]—Ver. 785. Colman observes: "Alluding to the money borrowed of her to pay Phormio; and as Donatus observes in another place, it is admirably contrived, in order to bring about a humorous catastrophe that Chremes should make use of his wife's money on this occasion."]

[Footnote 79: Our friend's]—Ver. 811. Chremes himself is so called, to deceive Nausistrata.]

[Footnote 80: O good luck]—Ver. 840. "Fors fortuna," "good fortune;" while "fortuna" merely means "chance."]

[Footnote 81: Throwing my cloak]—Ver. 843. When expedition was required, it was usual to throw the ends of the "pallium," or "cloak," over the shoulders.]

[Footnote 82: Carry me off]—Ver. 881. Madame Dacier says that Antipho is so rejoiced here at Geta's news, that he jumps upon his shoulders, and is carried off in triumph, which was a sort of stage-trick, and was very diverting to the Audience. On this, Colman observes: "I believe Madame Dacier has not the least foundation for this extraordinary piece of information; and I must confess, that I have too high an opinion, both of the Roman audience and actors, to believe it to be true."]

[Footnote 83: That as to what]—Ver. 898. Lemaire suggests that he is about to say: "that as to what was agreed upon between us, I may take home this young woman, and make her my wife."]

[Footnote 84: Is she not genteel-looking]—Ver. 904. Patrick has the following note here: "One can not conceive any thing more happy or just than these words of Chremes. Demipho's thoughts are wholly taken up how to recover the money, and Phormio is equally solicitous to retain it; but Chremes, who had just left his daughter, is regardless of their discourse, and fresh from the impressions which she had made on him, longs to know if his brother's sentiments of her were equally favorable, and naturally puts this paternal question to him."]

[Footnote 85: Transferred to my account]—Ver. 921. "Rescribere argentum," or "nummos," meant "to transfer," or "set down money to the account of another person in one's banker's books." A passage in the Asinaria of Plautus, l. 445, seems to have the same meaning.]

[Footnote 86: For the well portioned]—Ver. 939. Though Colman thinks otherwise, it is pretty clear that he alludes to Nausistrata in these words.]

[Footnote 87: To be carrying off]—Ver. 954. Patrick has the following note here: "The different characters of the two brothers are admirably preserved throughout this Scene. Chremes stands greatly in awe of his wife, and will submit to any thing rather than the story should come to her ears; but Demipho can not brook the thoughts of losing so much money, *and encourages his brother to behave with spirit and resolution, promising to make up matters between him and his wife."]*

[Footnote 88: Dead and gone]—Ver. 965. "E medio excedere," was an Euphemism signifying "to die," which it was deemed of ill omen to mention.]

[Footnote 89: Those who have]—Ver. 1025. He here uses the terms which it was customary to employ in the celebration of a public funeral. See also the form of proclaiming an auction, at the end of the Menæchmi of Plautus.]

[Footnote 90: Have him victimised]—Ver. 1027. "Mactatus" was the term applied to the pouring of wine and frankincense on the victim about to be sacrificed, on which it was said to be "magis auctus," "increased," or "amplified;" which, in time, became corrupted into the word "mactatus," or "mactus."]

[Footnote 91: Grant us your applause]—Ver. 1054. Thus concludes the last, and certainly not the least meritorious of the Plays of our Author; indeed, for genuine comic spirit, it may challenge comparison with the Eunuch, which is in general considered to be the best.]

Henry Thomas Riley (Translator)

Riley was born in June 1816, the only son of Henry Riley of Southwark, an ironmonger.

He was educated at Chatham House, Ramsgate, and at Charterhouse School. University was at Trinity College, Cambridge, but at the end of his first term he moved to Clare College where he was admitted on 17th December 1834 and elected a scholar on 24th January 1835.

He graduated B.A. in 1840.

Riley was called to the bar at the Inner Temple on 23rd November 1847, but early in life he worked for booksellers, editing and translating. These skills were to bring him perhaps the real jewels of his legacy with his translations of Terence, Ovid, Plautus and Lucan during the 1850's.

When the Royal Charter of April 1869 set up the Historical Manuscripts Commission he was engaged as an inspector and tasked with examining the archives of various municipal corporations, the muniments of the colleges at Oxford and Cambridge, and the documents in the registries of various bishops and chapters.

Henry Thomas Riley died at Hainault House, the Crescent, Selhurst, Croydon, on 14th April 1878, aged 61.

Terence – A Concise Bibliography

Andria (The Girl from Andros) (166 BC)
Hecyra (The Mother-in-Law) (165 BC)
Heauton Timorumenos (The Self-Tormentor) (163 BC)
Phormio (The Scheming Parasite) (161 BC)
Eunuchus (The Eunuch) (161 BC)
Adelphoe (The Brothers) (160 BC)

The first known printed edition of Terence appeared in Strasbourg in 1470.

www.ingramcontent.com/pod-product-compliance
Lightning Source LLC
Chambersburg PA
CBHW021935040426
42448CB00008B/1072